What people are sayir

Why Not Waste Tim

What a hunger this book has created in me! I haven't had this with God and I want it. This book is marvelous. I want to give copies to my friends.

Carol Moss

"Why Not Waste Time With God" made me reflect on my walk with God and reminded me of wanting a closer walk each day, and that comes by spending time with Him.

Up until now, I have been marginally comfortable with the time and methods that I spend with God. Reading "Why Not Waste Time With God" has prodded me into taking another look at these. I came away from reading your new book feeling that you were pushing my feet to the fire. Thanks.

Dr. Bill & Jackie Luehe

The Lord has been speaking to my heart a long time about spending intimate time with Him. You cannot know someone unless you spend time with them. Here is my takeaway message from "Why Not Waste Time With God": God wants us in his lap, close to His heart, listening to His voice and gently loving Him as He loves us. I felt inspired by this book and encouraged at the same time.

Cathy Sampson

I started reading your book, "Why Not Waste Time With God." I am on page 70 and cannot put it down. Throughout my reading a fire has begun to stir in me. I relate to a lot of things you said, such as not feeling worthy to be in the presence of God.

Ben Maxwell

This book has really brought me back into balance and has freed me up to listen and experience God's love and helped me understand who I am as His child. Anyone, no matter where they are in their Christian life, would benefit from reading this book.

"Why Not Waste Time With God" was so refreshing, I felt encouraged and uplifted.

Evelyn Freidt

"Why Not Waste Time With God" has added fuel to my fire. After reading the first chapter, I had to put the book down and go spend time with God. This book deals with the reality of who God is, and how to find the healing that I need to receive the Father's love. This book has given me a deeper hunger for God.

Tony Kim

The greatest life lesson from this book: "Knowing God is proud of me... That was a most encouraging thought."

Pat Rodden

WHY NOT WASTE TIME WITH GOD?

BY MICHAEL EVANS

Archer-Ellison Publishing Company
Winter Park, Florida

© 2003 by Michael Evans
Published by Archer-Ellison Publishing Company
P.O. Box 5795
Winter Park, FL 32793

Printed in the United States of America

ISBN - 1-57472-236-0

DEDICATION

To Jane, whose love for me is amazing.

Thank you.

TABLE OF CONTENTS

ACKNOWLEDGEMENTS

T he journey with our Father God, our Lord Jesus and His Holy Spirit continues and should deepen throughout our lifetime. I am not where I was ten years ago, I am not yet where I hope to be ten years from now. I couldn't possibly remember or list the names of all those whose personal journeys with the Lord have spoken into my life, but I am truly grateful to all of them.

Specifically in regards to this book:

My special thanks to Dr. Harold Helms and my wife Jane who read the manuscript as I wrote it, for their input and encouragement regarding content, Biblical accuracy and grammar. The many hours they spent helping me better express what I was trying to say were invaluable.

To Rick and Carolyn Pruett without whose help this book may not have been possible.

Thanks to my Pastor and friend James Ranger. His encouragement during the writing of this project and his prayers and friendship over the years have been both healing and inspiring. Also, I am deeply indebted to my close friend and spiritual mentor Dr.Francis MacNutt. It has been a privilege to know him, sit under his teaching and minister alongside of him. His humility and grace have taught me much about the love of the Father expressed in the flesh of a man.

I could not be where I now am without the valuable input into my life of men like my friend and former pastor Dr. John Lavender, the teaching I received sitting under John Wimber, or the books I have read by men such as Francis Frangipane, Brennan Manning, Henri Nouwen, and Richard Foster to name a few.

A profound note of thanks to my editor, Grace Sarber, whose expertise and gracious handling of the manuscript brought it together as an easily readable book.

As the full manuscript developed the following friends read it offering comments and objective criticisms for which I am grateful: Dr. Jack Bailey, Barbara Brown, Chris Burciaga, Jana Deem, Dan Divita, my son Joshua Evans, Rod Fink, Jim and Pat Fitzpatrick, Evelyn Freidt, Tony Kim, Howard Kliever, Jan Lockhart, Bill and Jackie Luehe, Mike and Cindy Maddy, Ben Maxwell, Carol Moss,Gail Preston, Pat Rodden, Kathy Sampson, Gary Tobin, Silver Veloz, Captain Lanell Wasington, and Bill and Joy Wright Jr. They all made suggestions, raised questions and offered encouraging words. Special appreciation to Nathan Sampson, a fellow traveler on this journey, for his enthusiasm and support.

I deeply appreciate my two dear friends who have been there to encourage and help in this process, Allen and Kim D'Angelo. The many hours they spent doing the cover design, layout and publication of this book made the final product all the more special because of their love for me and the extra effort and encouragement they gave me to "get this done." Though I never intended to do so, Allen always told me I was going to write another book.

Above all of these, to the Lord Himself that He chose to redeem us, love us, and have an intimate relationship with each of us.

PREFACE

ike Evans is a mature, wise counselor and gifted healer. He exudes a warm gentle spirit. His smile is infectious; his compassion is engaging. He is relaxed, humorous, and attentive. When he talks, he looks you right in the eye. He is, in John Wimber's phrase, "Naturally supernatural." Mike is a listener. He listens to us and, more importantly, he listens to God. This is what this book is about.

In writing "Why Not Waste Time With God?" Mike joins the current renaissance in spiritual disciplines among "empowered evangelicals," such as Richard Foster and Dallas Willard. Like them, he invites us into a life of intimacy with our Lord. To accomplish this Mike calls us to a significant shift in priorities and time commitments. Rather than "wasting" or spending time on lesser things, he invites us to give this to the God who loves us and who delights to have us linger in his presence. Mike's thesis is clear, "If I want to build an intimate relationship with God I must spend time with him."

This book is not a "how to" manual, although Mike shares his own journey and helps us immensely with ours. This book frames spiritual growth with God's heart, given in his Son and validated by His Spirit. As it deeply probes us, it demolishes our excuses and defenses against divine intimacy.

Mike demonstrates the personal values of drawing close to God, such as restoring our self-esteem and bringing a sense of well being into our lives. He also scatters telling quotes from spiritual pioneers throughout the book: Thomas Kelly, Julian of Norwich, Henri Nouwen, Thomas Merton, A. W. Tozer, to name a few.

This book is for those fed up with superficial evangelicalism and our fast-paced consumer society. It is also for those who have or want a spiritual hunger that only God can satisfy. It is for those willing to have a fresh self-encounter and a fresh God-encounter.

We all "waste" time on lesser things. Mike gives us a grace-based invitation to "waste" time on God and reap the personal and eternal benefits. This book will convince you of the value and take you on the journey. Read it and be prepared to have your life deepened and transformed. We are all in Mike's debt for opening God's heart to us in such a knowledgeable and alluring way.

Dr. Don Williams, Senior Pastor (Ret.)
La Jolla, California Vineyard

INTRODUCTION

This journey into deeper intimacy with God the Father became compelling for me after I "hit the wall." I was at a place in my life where there was no one to whom I could turn, no one who would understand what I was going through. Because of physical, emotional and spiritual exhaustion, I was unmotivated and uninterested in helping anybody with anything. My wife recognized the symptoms of burnout and wisely suggested I take some time off by myself, rest and decide what I was going to do.

About twenty minutes from my home is a canyon with a raging river running through it. In the beginning I simply would sit by this river. I did not read any inspiring books, listen to worship music, read my Bible or pray. I just sat. That is all I wanted to do and all I was emotionally capable of doing. Most of the time I would sit and stare off into space. After about six weeks of this my body began to feel rested. I started enjoying this time alone doing nothing. I began to notice and enjoy the beauty of nature around me. I connect well with God through nature, and before long God and I were talking again. Most importantly I was learning how to sit quietly and listen. The solitude was refreshing and stimulating. During this time God planted the seed that began to germinate and grow into a desire to spend significant time alone with Him. This time allowed me to step back, look at my world and see with new eyes the frantic pace at which we live.

So often, doing things for God leaves us little time with God. No wonder we get discouraged, burned out and want to drop out. No wonder our spiritual lives seem so ordinary and uninspiring. No wonder the world is unimpressed with our God. I began to see that many of us in this walk of faith are just as stressed and frantic as everyone else around us. The writing of this book is the result of the journey on which God has led me for the last couple of years. I have been learning that I must be intimately connected with God, and the only way to do this is to spend significant time with God.

It has been said, "He who would find God will find time." Like most of my contemporaries, for many years my journey with God consisted of going to church, singing a few songs, tithing a little, having some fun, praying and perhaps doing a few devotions. The time I spent in devotions, however, was just enough to help me not feel guilty about not spending much time with God in prayer or reading His Word.

Of course, church on Sunday mornings and Wednesday nights placed me in the really spiritual class. This was good for my ego, and I was certain it made God happy and kept me in his good graces. What more could He want?

After becoming a full-time associate pastor I became a little more serious about my walk with the Lord. I began to try to read through the One-Year Bible on a consistent daily basis. Or I would switch to Oswald Chambers' *My Utmost For His Highest*. This usually lasted about three to four months. After all, I had a lot of important work to do for the Lord. I actually did quite a bit of reading, but it was usually to prepare for a lesson or sermon. My prayer life was sporadic, and my prayers usually were composed of my delivering a list of needs and going merrily on my way. The stories of the great men of faith spending four to six hours a day in prayer were incomprehensible to me. How could one possibly be still for that long and do nothing but pray? I could not think of that much to pray about.

The idea of spending time with God just to listen and be with Him did not appeal to me. I had not grasped the simple concept that if you want to build an intimate relationship with God you must spend time with Him. I was deluded in thinking that since I was doing all these great things for God we had a good, close relationship. Along the way there were times when I felt "caught up" into the presence of God and did not want to leave. But after coming down from these mountaintop experiences, the daily grind of life would pull me back to reality and I would become caught up in the works mentality once again.

I viewed prayer and solitude with God as a waste of valuable time. I did not look forward to my prayer time with anticipation or excitement. Rather, it was with a sense of duty that I had to perform in order to remain on good terms with God. I could not understand why my walk with God seemed so ordinary. I thought I knew God but found out later that I knew about God, for only in the last few years have I begun to truly know God.

The journey that has brought me to where I am now began with music. I connect easily with God through worship music. I would often lie in bed at night listening to worship music. I found it relaxing and refreshing. For me, this was emotionally, intimately connecting with God. I would grab my cassette player, go back to the bedroom, close the door, put on my headphones and begin to sing along with the music.

Another part of this journey was intentionally finding a place to be alone where I could talk to God and pray without interruption. That is where my river came in. I would sneak off in the middle of the day to go up to this river sometimes just to get away from people and have some down time. I loved to sit by this river for hours. At first my priority was to rest, but then I found it to be a place where I could spend time with God. The solitude was not simply restful; it was renewing.

The biggest obstacle was feeling guilty because I was not "doing something." I felt like I was wasting valuable time. We are so driven in our culture, and especially in our church culture that we must be doing something in order for God to be pleased with us. The idea of simply being with Him-doing absolutely "nothing" but being with Him-was a tough one to overcome. Now, I cannot imagine not doing it. Some would say I am wasting time, but I have come to see it as crucial for survival. I now look forward with anticipation to our time together.

What started me on writing this book was a talk I gave on time we spend with God. Through preparation for that teaching, I began to really understand the superficial relationship I had with Him and how much of the Church is very superficial in its relationship. I wanted to explore how we as believers typically relate to our God and how to delve into a deeper relationship with Him. I wanted to know the benefits of going deeper with God. I realized that my own prayer life needed a lot of work and that my understanding of who I am and how much He loves me needed to grow.

Through this process, God has communicated His message to me: "Michael, I really love you. You do not have to prove anything to Me. I want you to trust Me. I have started you on this journey. I am pleased with how far you have come, but there is more I want to share with you. As you spend time with Me I will show you parts of Me that you have never seen before and take you deeper than you have ever dreamed of going. I will restore your passion and joy. I want more time with you."

Now He wants me to get this message across to others. As He led me to write this book, He told me, " You can write this in a way that will speak to people. Speak about the deepest yearnings of your heart, about trust, about hope, about love. Make it your journey because that is real to you.

There will be great satisfaction in this for you, because you have always admired writers and never felt you were good enough to do this. But I will help you, and through Me you will be able to say this in a way that will speak my heart and the importance of spending time with me. I want more time with my children."

Once you begin to spend time with God, a peace begins to settle over your whole being. You start to grasp how very special you are to Him. You begin to be able to pull back from the rat race. Your dependence for approval from man becomes less and less of an issue. The desire for the spotlight fades. You want to be alone because you start to hunger for and enjoy the solitude and silence. You really start to see, smell and hear the world around you. You begin to see others with new eyes. You gain an appreciation for every moment of every day. The fears attendant with the future become less and less. You gain a new, fresh passion for God and the things of God, a new level of peace and settledness in your spirit. You become more at peace with yourself. The haste and driven pace at which most of us live begins to lessen. You begin to realize that God's approval does not depend on what you do or do not do.

Time spent with God can consist of reading and praying, but it always includes sitting quietly doing nothing but listening. It is not hurried. I do not have anything to prove. Mostly I just "hang out" with God, enjoying His presence.

My prayer is that this book will give you the encouragement and freedom to waste some time with God, too. I encourage you to begin your own journey here. Seek Him. Learn to spend time with Him in silence, waiting on Him, listening to Him. I can promise you the results are well worth any sacrifice.

Wasting away,
Mike Evans

1

WAITING AND WASTING

I n our daily lives our time with God often can be insignificant or completely left out of our day. Let me give you an example. What does a typical believer do early in the morning to prepare for the day? He or she jumps up, perhaps grabs a cup of coffee, deals with the kids and breakfast and possibly sits down to carve out a short "time with God." This may include a reading from the Bible or a devotional book. That done, he or she lays out a prayer list, perhaps offering a prayer for another person or two, protection for self and family and a little guidance for the day. Having completed this, the believer is off to work. I admit this may be a bit simplified, but it is accurate. In my experience with believers around the world, the majority of us spend little time with God on a consistent, daily basis. That's sobering!

Even more sobering is that many of us think the hour or two we spend at church during a week is more than enough quality time to have an intimate relationship with God. Consider this: As a parent, how would you feel if during a typical seven-day week your grown child came to your house to spend an hour with you? And how would it make you feel if during that hour your child talked with you while reading the newspaper or watching a show on television? What if at the end of the hour he or she jumped up, gave you a hug, said, "See you next week," and headed out the door?

Assuming that's the only hour out of the entire week that you saw your child, would you be immensely pleased and thankful your child had spent some time with you? I suspect that while you would be happy to see him or her and grateful for what little time you did have, you also would be a little saddened. You wanted to share so much with your child, but there just was not enough time. Isn't this typical of how many of us relate to God?

Somewhere deep within do you long for-hunger for-a walk with God that is so rich and satisfying that you would give anything to have it? How do we lay hold of a life like this? How do we live a life of prayer without ceasing? How do we live a life of commitment and worship? How do we sing and dance as we bask within His love? How do we walk in the power and authority that is ours by inheritance?

Thomas Kelly answers these questions:

> *We begin to do this after months, weeks and years of practice. After lapses and failures, returning again and again to try to walk in the presence of God, trying to sense God in everything. In the ordinariness of life, in the days of dreariness and depression and frustration, when it goes well, and when it does not go well.[1]*

Could it conceivably be a waste to spend our time with God? For many of us, the time we spend with God is minimal. We want relationship, but we do not want it to take too much time. "After all, we say, it is not the quantity but the quality that's important!" We have heard, or even made, this statement many times in relation to spending time with our children. It is not true when applied to our children. It is not true when applied to our God.

WAITING IS HARD

Our prayer is often, "Lord, give me patience-and I want it right now!" We exist in a world of fast food, instant worldwide communication and freeway express lanes. Dutch Sheets said, "We do not wait well. We're into microwaving. God, on the other hand, is usually into marinating."[2] In this environment we are supposed to teach our children to be patient. RIGHT ! We would rather do anything than wait. In fact some of us would rather do the wrong thing than wait.

Waiting is the rule rather than the exception in life. But we are an impatient people. We even get upset waiting at stoplights.

I pass through a certain stoplight every day on my way to and from work. One day I was in a hurry and became quite irritable when I had to stop and wait for this light to change. I knew this had to be the longest stoplight in the entire city. It certainly was slowing down the important mission I was on, whatever that happened to be. In my irritation, I decided to time it.

Impatiently, I watched the second hand on my watch tick off a full sixty seconds before that light changed and it was my turn to move. As I shot across the intersection it hit me that I had been fussing and fuming over sitting still for sixty seconds. At that moment, God said to me; "Michael, you are letting that sixty seconds ruin your day! You cannot even sit still at a stoplight for sixty seconds without getting upset!" The absurdity of this whole scene made me laugh. I was not running late for anything except my self-imposed schedule.

For those of us who travel, one of the most frustrating experiences is dealing with the airlines. Once I was flying home from the Midwest. My last stop was in Phoenix, Arizona, where I would change planes for the short one-hour flight home to Bakersfield. Our plane had been held up 45 minutes, so we already were late coming into Phoenix. I expected my connection to be tight. However, this particular airline never left or arrived on time, so I was not too worried about it. The pilots made up some time during the flight, and we arrived only six minutes late. I hurried out of the plane, ran across the terminal and came to a skidding stop in front of the departure gate, thinking I was only six minutes late so it should not be a problem. The sweet, blonde-haired agent at the counter smiled and said; "I am sorry, but the plane has already gone. We knew you were coming but we could not hold the plane. You'll have to wait for the next one. It will leave in three hours."

I almost totally lost it. Fortunately I was wise enough to know that getting angry and yelling at the agent would accomplish nothing, so I turned around, murmuring under my breath and paced around the terminal like a caged animal. I mumbled to myself; "Your airline was 45 minutes late departing, I arrive six minutes late, and you could not wait six minutes for me to get off one of your stupid planes and onto another for a short one-hour flight home! Now I have to wait three hours in this stupid terminal, then another hour flying because you could not wait six minutes!" It is a good thing nobody heard me. I was really angry.

The more I walked and talked, the angrier I became. After pacing around this terminal about 45 minutes I decided I might as well sit down because nothing was going to change and I was not accomplishing anything except getting more upset. I slipped a disc player out of the backpack, put the earphones on and hit the play button. Guess which song came on? "Bridge over Troubled Water," by Simon & Garfunkel.

> *"When you're weary, feeling small, when tears are in your eyes I'll dry them all. I'm on your side when times get rough and friends just can't be found. Like a bridge over troubled waters I will lay me down."*[3]

I started laughing at the absurdity of my anger. It was as if God was saying to me, "Would you look at yourself? You're acting like a spoiled little kid over something that is so minor. Get over it."

On another occasion, my wife Jane and I were on a plane that was delayed due to weather and sitting at the departure gate. After a long wait the pilots offered for us to switch to the plane sitting next to ours. It would be leaving soon and eventually get us where we needed to be. I was ready to get off that plane and go anywhere, but Jane's common sense and patience prevailed. It took every bit of self-restraint I could muster to sit and watch other people leave, assuming they would be long gone and we would still be sitting here on this plane.

Shortly after some of the passengers departed the plane, the captain said we had been cleared for takeoff. The other plane was still sitting there at the gate as we taxied by, smiling and waving. When we arrived at our destination and went to the next departure gate the gate attendant informed us that they thought we had gotten off the plane at the last stop and had given our seats to someone else! I was really cool. Honest! First she said we would have to wait for another plane, which would be several hours. Then she said, "Why don't you just hang around for a little bit, and we'll see what we can do." As we sat there patiently waiting, they loaded the plane with all the passengers and then called our names. The lady at the desk said, "We have a couple of seats in First Class. If that's okay, you can have those." You do not have to be a rocket scientist to know how to answer this question.

Maybe for you it is a simple, everyday occurrence like going to the grocery store. Do you find that when you are ready to check out you start looking for the shortest line? You pick one and stand in it for a minute, but you see one that is shorter so you go over to that line. Inevitably, after you are already in line, the person in front of you pulls out a fistful of coupons and starts rummaging around looking for his or her checkbook, identification or store discount card! You longingly look over at the line you just left and know that if you had stayed in that line you would already be in your car, groceries in the trunk, satisfied at having completed another harrowing mission. It drives you nuts, right?

We are a busy people, harried and hurried through each day. We are well acquainted with doing things for God, rather than sitting with Him and doing nothing. When asked to consider the disciplines of silence, solitude or stillness, many of us may respond by saying, "We do not have time." For most of us, waiting is a difficult task.

In *A Testament of Devotion* Thomas Kelly writes:

> *"Our lives in a modern city grow too complex and overcrowded. Even the necessary obligations which we feel we must meet grow overnight, like Jack's beanstalk, and before we know it we are bowed down with burdens, crushed under committees, strained, breathless and hurried, panting through a never-ending program of appointments. We are too busy to be good wives to our husbands, good homemakers, good companions of our children, good friends to our friends, and with no time at all to be friends to the friendless.*
>
> *But if we withdraw from public engagements and interests, in order to spend quiet hours with the family, the guilty calls of citizenship whisper disquieting claims in our ears. Our children's schools should receive our interest, the civic problems of our community need our attention, the wider issues of the nation and of the world are heavy upon us. Our professional status, our social obligations, our membership in this or that very important organization put claims upon us. And in frantic fidelity we try to meet at least the necessary minimum of calls upon us. But we're weary and breathless. And we know and regret that our life is slipping away, with our having tasted so little of the peace and joy and serenity we are persuaded it should yield to a soul of wide caliber. The times for the deeps of the silences of the heart seem so few.*
>
> *And in guilty regret we must postpone till next week that deeper life of unshaken composure in the holy Presence, where we sincerely know our true home is, for this week is much too full."[4]*

We would never actually admit we do not have time for God, but our daily lives demonstrate that we take little of the time we do have to be with God. We may even think we would be wasting our valuable time by spending it in prayer, silence or solitude.

WHY WOULD WE WANT TO WAIT?

Waiting often brings about guilt. We have this nagging feeling that we are being selfish, wasting time, evading the responsibilities of family, career or ministry. This idleness is a luxury, and we cannot afford it.

Part of why we feel guilty is that we do not fully know the God with whom we are spending time! We would not feel guilty spending time with a brilliant scientist or a famous author or a world-renowned artist, so why would we not want to spend time with the God who made it all? If we truly understood that the God of the universe, the God who made everything that is, wants to spend time with us, we would do anything, give up anything, go anywhere to be with Him.

Unfortunately, it is hard for us to grasp this reality because so few of us have ever had anybody love us the way He loves us. We even may feel unconsciously as if we do not deserve to take His time. We feel as if He has so many important things to do that we are wasting His time! Know what? He wants to waste time with us!

Spending time with God means learning to trust, surrender and wait. "Yet those who wait for the Lord will gain new strength; they will mount up with wings like eagles, they will run and not get tired, they will walk and not become weary" (Isaiah 40:31). "For the Lord is a God of justice. Blessed are all who wait for Him!" (Isaiah 30:18).

Scripture indicates that He longs to be gracious to us, desires to show us His compassion. For this to happen we not only must learn to wait but also to be separate. "'Therefore, come out from their midst and be separate,' says the Lord. 'And do not touch what is unclean; and I will welcome you. And I will be a father to you, and you shall be sons and daughters to Me,' says the Lord Almighty. Therefore, having these promises, beloved, let us cleanse ourselves from all defilement of flesh and spirit, perfecting holiness in the fear of God" (2 Corinthians 6: 17-7:1,NAS).

To wait and to come out are contrary to our normal way of life. But if we are going to be with God in an intimate, nurturing, growing relationship, we must spend significant time with Him. Theologian Edward Schillebeeckx succinctly stated the bottom-line reason for waiting on the Lord: "In a revealed religion, silence with God has value in itself and for its own sake, just because God is God. Failure to recognize the value of mere being with God, as the beloved, without doing anything, is to gouge the heart out of Christianity."[5]

CATCHING THE WAVES

Most of us have read or heard about men and women like St. Francis of Assisi, Thomas Merton, St. Teresa of Avila, Thomas Kempis or Brother Lawrence who spent hours and hours in prayer and solitude, worshipping and listening to God. We may be awed, inspired or discouraged by these stories. Typically we respond, "I could never do that! How could I possibly sit still for that long doing absolutely nothing? I cannot even get my mind to be quiet for two to three minutes of prayer. I cannot imagine an hour or a day, much less several days, of quiet solitude."

Such practices are foreign to us, shrouded with cloaks of mystery or mysticism, and we ignore them because of ignorance or fear. When people talk to us about the disciplines of the inner life, practicing the perpetual return of the soul into the inner sanctuary, or being alone with the Alone, we might respond by saying, "That sounds like Eastern Mysticism, or that is obviously New Age teaching, and we certainly do not want to go there." Or our response is, "I don't have time for that. That's wasting time, and I really need to be doing something for God." That is what we know. That is what we do best. We try to make things happen!

Even the Church says to us, "Get involved. Do something."

So instead, we rush to read the latest book or attend the latest conference. Numerous Christian conferences specialize on the "how tos" of a successful, joyful, prosperous life. But when was the last time you went to a conference or workshop on "How to Practice Solitude," or "The Power of Silence and Meditation in Your Time with God," or even "Getting In Touch With The Core of Your Soul"?

Our spiritual life moves in waves, and we try to catch the next wave, moving from the top of one to the next. We catch the wave of Authority and then move to the wave of Territorial Warfare, then the wave of Intercessory Prayer, then the wave of the Prophetic, then the wave of the Apostolic Anointing. All of these we frantically run after, looking for something more-desiring, hungering, thirsting, but deep within always missing the very intimacy with God that our hearts truly seek.

Brennan Manning sums up best what seems to be the normal questions asked among believers after the excitement and emotional high of their salvation experience has settled into the routine of daily life. He asks, "Have you ever felt baffled by your internal resistance to prayer? By the existential dread of silence, solitude and being alone with God? By the way you drag yourself out of bed for morning praise, shuffle off to worship with the sacramental slump of the terminally ill, endure nightly prayer with stoic resignation, knowing that "this too shall pass?"[6]

The ideas of contemplation, meditation, silence or solitude are not only foreign to us but even seem threatening. We dread being alone with God because it requires a level of intimacy we fear.

INTIMACY

My wife and I have a relationship of openness and transparency. I enjoy being with her. Through a marriage of 31 years, our relationship has grown more intimate, our friendship deeper and our love for each other stronger. I do not resist being with her. If I have to be away because of traveling, I miss her and cannot wait to return home. I suppose many of you have this same type of relationship with your spouse, but how many of us have a similar relationship with God?

Intimacy by necessity requires commitment, honesty and transparency-and that's scary! Transparency involves risk, and risk opens us up to wounding. And if people have been wounded in the past by others who claim to love them, how can they be sure it will not happen again if they open themselves up to a God whom they are not convinced they can trust?

Church is a place for fellowship with God and other believers, and there are times when we need to be in an attitude of respect and awe of God. But intimacy with God is what it is all about. My experience with intimacy is that there are moments of incredible delight and fun, and there are quiet moments when no words are necessary.

By its very definition intimacy denotes relationship with a close friend or confidante. When I am around a close friend I do not have to pretend. I can be myself, totally open and free. A quotation from C. Raymond Beran about friendship has helped me define a friend.

> *WHAT IS A FRIEND?*
> *I will tell you. It is a person with whom you dare to be yourself. Your soul can be naked with him. He seems to ask of you to put on nothing; only be what you are. He does not want you to be better or worse. When you are with him, you feel as a prisoner feels who has been declared innocent. You do not have to be on your guard. You can say what you think, so long as it is genuinely you. He understands those contradictions in your nature that lead others to misjudge you. With him you breathe freely. You can avow your little vanities and envies and hates and vicious sparks, your meannesses and absurdities and, in opening them up to him they are lost, dissolved on the white ocean of his loyalty. He understands. You do not have to be careful. You can abuse him, neglect him, tolerate him. Best of all, you can*

keep still with him. It makes no matter. He likes you. He is like fire that purges to the bone. He understands. He understands. You can weep with him, sin with him, laugh with him, pray with him. Through it all-and underneath-he sees, knows and loves you. A friend? What is a friend? Just one, I repeat, with whom you dare to be yourself.[7]

While I hunger to have an intimate relationship with God as Abba or Daddy, I also need to see Him as Friend. One with whom I can be myself and know that He understands and accepts me in all my humanness.

When I understand that He accepts me, then I can begin to grasp my uniqueness and destiny as a child of eternity. In *A Testament of Devotion*, Thomas Kelly writes:

Deep within us all there is an amazing inner sanctuary of the soul, a holy place, a Divine Center, a speaking Voice to which we may continuously return. Eternity is at our hearts, pressing upon our time-worn lives, warming us with intimations of an astounding destiny, calling us home unto Itself. Yielding to these persuasions, gladly committing ourselves in body and soul, utterly and completely, to the Light Within, is the beginning of true life.[8]

FROM FIERY PASSION TO SMOLDERING ASHES

Lloyd Ogilvie wrote, "We were created for an intimate relationship with God and one another."[9] Do you remember the earliest stage of your Christian walk, with its boundless excitement and feeling of joy and power? You felt invincible! You felt there was nothing you and God together could not do. Your newfound passion and devotion changed how you related to everything around you. You looked for opportunities to share this Good News with anyone who would listen and some who would not. You attacked your Bible with the fervor of a man who had been lost in the desert and had suddenly come upon a sparkling spring of cool, clear water.

But as time elapsed, though you are not certain when or how, something happened, and the fire and passion died.

Your exciting new relationship with God, which you had enjoyed while praying, reading His Word, attending worship services, and witnessing became no more than ritualistic behavior. The intimacy and joy were gone. The fires of newfound passion were reduced to smoldering ashes. Instead of stirring us to draw nearer to God, our brokenness often drives us into despair. Julian of Norwich said, "Our courteous Lord does not want his servants to despair because they fall often and grievously; for our falling does not hinder Him in loving us." [10] Possibly our falling hinders us because we let it hinder us, and we project onto God how we feel about ourselves.

For some, comparison becomes the norm. We compare our Christian lives with that of other believers. We base our value on how much we read Scripture, pray, witness or give of our time and money. Unfortunately, such comparisons do not inspire us to new heights. We find it difficult to accept that "God is relentlessly tender and compassionate toward us just as we are-not in spite of our sins and faults (that would not be total acceptance), but with them. Though God does not condone or sanction evil, He does not withhold His love because there is evil in us." [11]

Perhaps you find yourself feeling guilty or stifled because of your inability to develop intimacy with the Lord. The "I shoulds" plague you-I should witness, I should obey God's rules, I should read the Bible, pray, tithe and attend church. Guilt and regret set in when you find it difficult, if not impossible, to live up to these demands. As you read the Bible, or heard solid biblical teaching, you become aware that you fall far short of these standards. In fact, instead of bringing freedom, the Law brings you under bondage. Thoughts like, "I can never measure up," or "I do not feel like a very good Christian," begin to discourage you.

Perhaps you are encouraged by things that generally work for short periods of time, such as a great sermon, a good book, or an encouraging word from a friend. However, before long thoughts or behaviors begin to appear that may include a burning desire to please the Lord but also a fear that whatever you are doing isn't quite good enough. You find yourself growing frustrated and angry with the Christian life. You experience a gnawing discomfort that you do not have the power within yourself to live up to the standards. Suddenly it is not as much fun as it used to be. The joy is gone, and you feel weighed down.

At some point you may ask yourself how this could have happened. You, like all of us, want those desires that the Holy Spirit stirs within us. You want to experience again the yearning for that river of living water that can flow from deep within. How do we turn this extrinsic motivation (motivation outside ourselves to do things), into intrinsic motivation (motivation from within)?

IMPEDIMENTS TO INTIMACY

What often hinders our intimacy with God is the same thing that hinders our intimacy with people. We pretend everything is okay when it is not okay. We easily fool those around us. We can be an emotional mess inside, but on the outside we have a happy face that says we are at peace. Our outward appearance says; "It is well with my soul. Life could not be any better." How many times have people asked, "How are you doing?" and you responded, "Great!" Inside you were feeling rotten, but you did not want to bother going into the whole story because you knew they did not want to know, nor could they do anything about it.

I read a story involving some American soldiers during the Korean War. They rented a house and hired a local Korean to do their housekeeping and cooking. It was common during that war for soldiers to get that kind of setup for easy-come, easy-go, easy-pay. The Korean fellow they hired had an unbelievable positive attitude. He was always smiling. So they played one trick after another on him. They nailed his shoes to the floor. He would get up in the morning, pull those nails out with pliers, slip on the shoes and maintain his excellent spirit. They put grease on the stove handles, and he would wipe each one off, smiling and singing his way through the day. They balanced buckets of water over the door, and he would get drenched. But he would dry off and never fuss, time after time. Finally, they became so ashamed of themselves that they called him in one day and said, "We want you to know that we're never going to trick you again. Your attitude has been outstanding." He asked, "You're not going to nail my shoes to the floor?" "We're not." "You'll stop smearing grease on the stove knobs?" "Yes." "No more water buckets over the door?" "No more." "Okay, then I'll stop spitting in the soup!" It is easy to do that, isn't it? We say with our faces that we are doing well, but we are fretting and hiding the problems and refusing to deal with the issues. We are "spitting in the soup" more often than not!

We are the greatest impediment to our intimacy with God. We often respond to God as we respond to people. Since we think we will be accepted and loved only if we perform acceptably, we pretend, thus preventing fellowship with others and blocking whatever God would do to transform our defeats into victories.

"Doing"

After becoming believers, "doing" becomes the measure of our growth and acceptance. We have the life-giving message of Jesus for salvation, but we believe we need Jesus *plus*-Jesus *plus* the Law, Jesus *plus* circumcision, Jesus *plus* abstaining from meat sacrificed to idols.

Paul addressed this false belief: "You foolish Galatians, who has bewitched you, before whose eyes Jesus Christ was publicly portrayed as crucified? This is the only thing I want to find out from you: did you receive the Spirit by the works of the Law, or by hearing with faith? Are you so foolish? Having begun by the Spirit, are you now being perfected by the flesh?"(Galatians 3:1-3).

Could Paul be saying to give up? To give up your efforts at trying to please God in the power of your flesh? Activity is not bad, in and of itself, but tragically little emphasis is spent on such disciplines as solitude, meditation and silence. This can result in a lack of power that manifests itself in a dull, bland, compromised life. This means that we have lost our intimacy, our first love.

Fearing Rejection

Sometimes we believe that He will love us only if we are good, so we pretend we are something we are not. We put up a facade of rightness while, in reality, we are a tangled mess of fears and frustrations. We may even claim to be okay and try to hide from Him those parts of ourselves that we believe will cause Him to reject and abandon us.

All the while, the Lord desires to go beneath the surface to the real person living inside our skin. We can profess Christ as Savior while denying Him lordship of our innermost thoughts, dreams and plans. We are deceived by the subtle belief that somehow we must make ourselves acceptable to God, that God will refuse to accept us as we are in our sinful humanity and depravity.

In many ways we are like the leper in Mark, "A man with leprosy came to him and begged him on his knees, "If you are willing, you can make me clean" (Mark 1:40). Leprosy separated its victims from the rest of society. No one wanted to be in the vicinity of someone with leprosy. It was a dreaded disease with fearsome consequences. It was seen as a sign of defilement and uncleanness on one who had displeased God. Since God had rejected the leper, the Jews could reject them also. When the leper came to Jesus, his greatest fear was rejection. His friends and family had rejected him. It may have been years since he had felt the touch of another human being. How long had it been since he felt the touch of a wife or his little child? People would pull back in horror as he approached.

Likewise, we often feel that our sin has defiled us so that we can no longer come into the presence of a holy God. We believe that He will pull back, turn from us or abandon us, just like everyone else, because we are defiled or have not been able to live up to His standards. We know God can heal us, but we are not sure He will. Or, we know He loves us, but we need to get ourselves cleaned up before we come to Him.

We try to hide from God because of self-rejection. We think to ourselves what Henri Nouwen eloquently expressed: "As soon as someone accuses me or criticizes me, as soon as I am rejected, left alone or abandoned, I find myself thinking, 'Well, that proves once again that I am nobody.'"[12] "Self-rejection is the greatest enemy of the spiritual life because it contradicts the sacred voice that calls us the 'Beloved.' Being the Beloved constitutes the core truth of our existence."[13]

If we cannot accept ourselves in both our strengths and weaknesses, we cannot accept that we are of value to God. To grasp the reality of being the Beloved is totally beyond our reach.

One of the most well known parables in the Bible is found in Luke 15. It is the parable of the Prodigal Son, who left his home and squandered his inheritance while living a life of sin and self-gratification. In so doing, he experienced life's harshness, cruelty and suffering. When he decided to return to his father's house, the father saw him coming and in compassion ran to meet him. He embraced, accepted and forgave him before the son even had an opportunity to say he was sorry. Though the son was not sure how his father would respond, he was certain of one thing, the father loved him.

God has not changed. He wants to love, accept, heal and forgive us. Because of our experiences or circumstances, we find it hard to comprehend that He will never reject us. Grasp this: God will always reach across the chasm that separates us and will embrace us. His love is totally beyond our comprehension and understanding.

Walking in Darkness

We must clearly understand that any sin we commit defiles us. Whether it is anger, resentment, judgment, gossip, lying or any one of a multitude of sins listed in the Bible, it defiles us.

> *"This is the message we have heard from Him and declare to you: God is light; in Him there is no darkness at all. If we claim to have fellowship with Him yet walk in the darkness, we lie and do not live by the truth. But if we walk in the light, as He is in the light, we have fellowship with one another, and the blood of Jesus, His Son, purifies us from all sin. If we claim to be without sin, we deceive ourselves and the truth is not in us. If we confess our sins, He is faithful and just and will forgive us our sins and purify us from all unrighteousness. If we claim we have not sinned, we make Him out to be a liar and His word has no place in our lives.* 1 John 1:5-10*

Walking in darkness is not allowing His transforming power and light into our lives. It is not allowing the Lord's light of truth to reveal any area of our lives not surrendered to Him. Intimacy is rooted in honesty. Honesty with God invites Him to take charge of all our relationships and dreams. If our careers, money, self-image, hopes, disappointments and goals have never been submitted to Him, our Christianity is a mere shell of what it was meant to be.

RECOVERING INTIMACY

Most likely we were not aware that development and growth in this relationship with God required honesty, openness and trust. Because deep intimacy with God is so foreign and contradictory to how we generally live, we also did not understand that this relationship requires significant time.

Giving up the "Doing"

God does not want your good works as much as He wants you. Allow God to convince you that He loves you. Allow Him to teach you that He is ultimately responsible for your spiritual growth. "For I am confident of this very thing, that He who began a good work in you will perfect it until the day of Christ Jesus" (Philippians 1:6).

Give up the works of the flesh. He will give you the desire to pray, the discipline to stick to it, the self-control to say no to distractions. Give up and give yourself, all you know and all you have to God. We need His love to permeate and saturate our lives so that we may be healed, restored and renewed.

Overcoming Rejection

It begins with ruthless, naked trust. Thomas Merton says this, "Surrender your poverty and acknowledge your nothingness to the Lord. Whether you understand it or not, God loves you, is present in you, lives in you, dwells in you, calls you, saves you and offers you an understanding and compassion which are like nothing you have ever found in a book or heard in a sermon." [14]

Have I allowed God to know me absolutely and utterly? Does He know my plans, dreams, feelings and attitudes about people and life? If not, why not? Is it because I fear He will reject me or find me unworthy? Some ask, "Doesn't he already know all there is to know about me?" Of course! Well then, why do we need to expose ourselves to him? Because when you, by a direct act of the will, choose to expose and surrender those areas to God, you are freeing yourself from the burden of guilt and change.

There comes a time when we cannot say we love God and exclude him from the real person inside this flesh. Until we allow Him access to the nerve center of our secret thoughts and feelings, our intimacy will be fleeting. If we confess whatever it is in us that keeps us from the intimacy we were created to experience, forgiveness is immediate! Imagine the tragedy of living your whole life under the burdens of guilt, shame and anger when the experience of liberating love and forgiveness is so easily obtained. God will not ever give up on you.

Walking in the Light

"If we walk in the light as He Himself is in the light, we have fellowship with one another, and the blood of Jesus His Son cleanses us from all sin. If we say that we have no sin, we are deceiving ourselves, and the truth is not in us. If we confess our sins, He is faithful and righteous to forgive us our sins and to cleanse us from all unrighteousness" (1 John 1:7,8)

It is kind of like sitting around cursing the darkness when all you need to do is light a candle! Intimacy requires that we be vulnerable, exposed and naked. It requires that we be accountable. Most of us do not like being accountable. We often prefer a more casual, "How you doing?" kind of relationship. But those kinds of relationships do not produce growth or change. They produce sameness, lukewarmness and shallowness. Growth in our spiritual life begins when we accept that we are a broken, wounded people, loved by God in our broken, wounded condition. Just like Adam and Eve, we were created for intimacy with God, but when we hide from Him our relationship is damaged and His heart is broken.

WAITING ON GOD

We are especially impatient when it comes to waiting. "Wait before the Lord in silence." In silence? Are you kidding? I need to be doing something and I do not like silence. I cannot just stand here waiting-what a waste of time!

When I teach on the topic of praying for healing; I use a teaching model that emphasizes waiting for the Holy Spirit to show us how He wants us to pray before actually beginning to pray with someone. This means that we wait quietly for a short time before we actually start praying.

Someone said to me once; "We do not have time for all this waiting. We have too many people to pray for!" I could not believe it. We are praying to God, asking Him to tell us how He wants us to pray, and we do not have time to wait for Him to tell us! It is not that we do not know how to pray. Rather, we do not want to take the time to wait and listen.

I often tell people that the most difficult thing they will do when praying for someone is to wait and listen. Why would you pray for someone without knowing what God wants you to pray? Why would you ask God to give you an answer on something and then not wait for Him to give it! That is like spitting into the wind. You do not have to do it many times before you realize it is not very smart.

WASTING TIME WITH HIM

Why "waste time" with God?

Why is this necessary?

Well, for starters, peace begins to settle over your whole being.

You become more at peace with yourself, and you experience a settledness in your spirit.

You start to grasp how very special you are to Him.

You begin to realize that God's approval does not depend on what you do or do not do. You begin to be able to pull back from the rat race. The haste and driven pace at which most of us live begins to lessen.

Fears about the future become significantly less.

You are able to break free from dependence on others for approval. Your desire for the spotlight fades.

You want to be alone because you start to hunger for and enjoy the solitude and silence. You actually start to see, smell and hear the world around you. You begin to see others with new eyes. You gain an appreciation for every moment of every day.

You gain a new and fresh passion for God and the things of God.

You learn to love more compassionately, give of yourself more freely and take yourself less seriously.

You can stop your pretense and striving for approval, and instead, sitting quietly with your Father God, you can be confident that you are significant, accepted and loved.

Are you tired of seeking approval in superficial relationships? Do you long to experience the intimacy, joy and freedom that can come when you are deeply connected, soul and spirit, with your Father God? If so, you must prepare yourself to waste some time with God.

2

The Value of Nurturing the Soul

D
o you really want to live your life-every moment of your life-in His presence? Do you long for Him, thirst for Him? Do you hunger to be in His presence? "Do you want to live in such an amazing divine Presence that life is transformed and transfigured and transmuted into peace and power and glory and miracle?"[1]

If you do, then you can. But most of us may believe we do not have the time to submit to the silence and solitude that is re-creative. Life is too busy with spouse, kids, job, school, friends or fun. Most likely, you are not ready to go that deep yet. You do not at this point love God above all else in the world. You do not yet love Him with all your heart, soul, mind and strength. But Scripture tells us that this is what His heart longs of us.

Is it not true that whenever we really want to do something we find time to do it? It is not so much that we lack the time, but the discipline. And we lack the joy of knowing the inexpressible delight of being with the Father God because we so seldom go there for any length of time. When we read, "My soul pants for Thee" (Psalm 42:1), we may realize that we do pant, but not for God. Instead, in our feverish scrambling, we long and pant after other things. We run after security, success, the latest fad, a new way to pray, a new way to spend a minute with God.

A..W. Tozer wrote:

> *"In my creature impatience I am often caused to wish that there were some way to bring modern Christians into a deeper spiritual life painlessly by short easy lessons; but such wishes are vain. No shortcut exists. God has not bowed to our nervous haste nor embraced the methods of our machine age. It is well that we accept the hard truth now: the man who would know God must give time to Him. He must count no time wasted that is spent in the cultivation of His acquaintance. He must give himself to meditation and prayer hours on end."[2]*

But in addition to a lack of discipline and lack of knowing the joy of being with the Father, what many of us lack is a nurturing relationship with God. Nurturing allows us to speak and act from strength rather than from fear or insecurity. It helps us to begin to understand our true value and worth, to get in touch with our "belovedness." Knowing our value and worth frees us from dependence on other people. It allows us to experience the profound, daily joy of just being alive. We do not have to justify ourselves or apologize for being alive. We can enjoy simply being.

Most importantly, a nurturing relationship with the Father allows us to hear this message: *It is okay to do nothing but sit quietly in His presence. God still loves you! You do not have to always do something for Him.*

WHAT WE SEE IN THE MIRROR

When you look at yourself, what do you see? Do you like what you see? At some point you might have said things about yourself like, "I hate myself!" "I do not like my nose, legs, etc." "I am not wanted." "I am so clumsy I cannot do anything right." "I am not good enough to be accepted and forgiven by God." "I wish I were a boy/girl." Such statements are typical of those who have little self-esteem, whose self-image is deeply wounded, who feel like a flawed clay pot rather than a treasure.

Many of us have an intense dislike of ourselves and project onto Jesus our own feelings about ourselves. We decide that if we cannot accept what we perceive as flaws, than neither can Jesus. Though we cannot blame Satan for our weaknesses and failures, we must recognize that he lurks in the background, ready and waiting to take advantage of whatever is there, to harass and, if possible, destroy us.

David Seamands wrote:

> *"They find themselves defeated by the most psychological weapon that Satan uses against Christians. This weapon has the effectiveness of a deadly missile. Its name? Low self-esteem. Satan's greatest psychological weapon is a gut-level feeling of inferiority, inadequacy and low self-worth. This feeling shackles many Christians, in spite of wonderful spiritual experiences, in spite of their faith and knowledge of God's Word. Although they understand their position as sons and daughters of God, they are tied up in knots, bound by a terrible feeling of inferiority, and chained to a deep sense of worthlessness."[3]*

In my youth, I continually heard sermons emphasizing hell. They pretty well convinced me that all those things I wanted to do were sinful, and that even thinking about such things meant I was bad. They drummed into me that God was going to get me if I did anything wrong. Instead of seeing myself as a person of value to God, I thought God was incessantly watching and waiting to catch me doing something wrong. No wonder I grew up thinking God was there to spoil my fun. With such a church background combined with what was happening in my life as I entered adolescence, my self-image was shaky.

During my junior high and high school days my family

was not only deeply involved in church activities where I heard all this hellfire and brimstone preaching, but my hormones were kicking in, making me an adolescent mess. Physically, I was a small, uncoordinated guy. I remember standing in line during physical education class waiting to be chosen for a team. When it came time to be chosen for a team, I was the one left over. The team captains would argue over who would have to have me on their team. All this reinforced this short, skinny, uncoordinated kid's sense of inadequacy. I wanted to play sports, but I was too short for basketball, too little for football and too uncoordinated for baseball. I overcame this lack of athletic prowess by joining the high school choir. But, of course, since our school was ruled by jocks this really did not help much in pursuing a status as a big man on campus.

I also grew up in a family of hunters and, though I did not particularly like hunting, it was the manly thing to do. All the men in my family hunted. In order to participate in male bonding, I had to hunt. I will never forget my first hunting experience. We were out on the opening day of dove season. I had a shotgun, which weighed about as much as I did, and a bird was unlucky enough to fly over my head. I shot and hit the bird, and we all ran over to where it lay. Unfortunately, I had merely wounded it, and the bird was lying there on the ground bleeding, flapping its wings looking up at me with these pleading eyes. I looked down at this bird and felt horrible. But, of course, all my relatives were congratulating me on what a great hunter I was going to be. On the outside I appeared quite manly and proud of myself, but I was crying on the inside and thinking there must be something wrong with me. Why did I not feel good about myself when my dad was obviously proud of me?

Not until the latter part of my college years did I discover some sports I could do well. Skiing and sailing were two of these. I became an avid snow skier. What that did for my self-image is beyond words. It was also during these latter years of college that I began to learn I was of value to God. I began to understand that I was of great worth and significance. I actually began to receive positive input from people and started feeling that I might be okay.

TREASURE IN JARS OF CLAY

Though we are flawed vessels, with cracks and imperfections, Paul tells us that within this earthen jar lies a priceless treasure. "But we have this treasure in jars of clay to show that this all-surpassing power is from God and not from us" (2 Corinthians 4:7). The treasure is not a power in ourselves, but the incomparable power of the living God. It is not there because of anything we do, but rather because of what God has done in us.

Unfortunately we often focus on our flaws, and consequently we allow these flaws to prevent us from seeing ourselves as God sees us. When God looks at us He looks past the flaws and sees the treasure. This treasure is the power of God-a power that is not to be ignored or hidden away. Rather, it is to be used to reveal God to others. Without an intimate, nurturing relationship with God we will not be able to see past the flaws of the vessel that carries this treasure, and we will miss the very purpose God deposited it in us. Once we grasp what a treasure God deposited in this earthen vessel, we will understand that God will use these imperfections to bring good, light and even life..

This story was sent to me via e-mail. I do not know the source, but it beautifully illustrates how God uses our flaws to bring life and light to others.

> *"A water bearer in India had two large pots, which he hung on each end of a pole that he carried across his neck. One of the pots had a crack in it. While the other pot was perfect and always delivered a full portion of water at the end of the long walk from the stream to the master's house, the cracked pot arrived only half full. For a full two years the bearer daily delivered only one and a half pots full of water to his master's house. Of course, the perfect pot was proud of its accomplishments, perfectly fulfilling the purpose for*

which it was made. But the poor cracked pot was ashamed of its imperfection and miserable that it was able to accomplish only half of what it had been made to do.

After two years of what it perceived to be bitter failure, it spoke to the water bearer one day by the stream. "I am ashamed of myself, and I want to apologize to you."

"Why?" asked the bearer. "What are you ashamed of?"

"For these past two years I have been able to deliver only half of my load because this crack in my side causes water to leak out all the way back to your master's house. Because of my flaws, you have to do all of this work, and you do not get full value from your efforts," the pot said.

The water bearer felt sorry for the old cracked pot, and in his compassion he said, "As we return to the master's house, I want you to notice the beautiful flowers along the path." Indeed, as they went up the hill, the old cracked pot took notice of the beautiful flowers on the side of the path, and this cheered it some. But at the end of the trail, it still felt bad because it had leaked out half its load, and so again it apologized to the bearer for its failure.

The bearer said to the pot, "Did you notice that there were flowers only on your side of the path, but not on the other pot's side? That's because I have always known about your flaw, and I took advantage of it. I planted flower seeds on your side of the path, and every day as we walked back from the stream, you've watered them. For two years I have been able to pick these beautiful flowers to decorate my master's table. Without your being just the way you are, he would not have this beauty to grace his house."

Each of us has his own unique flaws. In some ways we are all like cracked pots. (As I think about it, I have even been referred to on occasion as a "crackpot.") We are all born in sin, but we are treasures that can reflect His goodness. God sees us from a perspective that we do not, and in His infinite love He uses what we see as flaws to bring life and beauty to those around us.

Of course, we are a wounded people. We may have grown up in families where we were deeply wounded by something that was said to us. Perhaps we went to schools where our looks or our lack of athletic ability embarrassed us. Maybe we have accepted the notion that we are of little value and have little to give. That is exactly where the enemy would like to keep us, if we let him. However, that is not the image the Bible illustrates.

GOD MADE US OF IMMENSE WORTH AND VALUE

The Bible constantly affirms that human beings are valuable in God's sight: "But you are a chosen race, a royal priesthood, a holy nation, a people for God's own possession, that you may proclaim the excellencies of Him who has called you out of darkness into His marvelous light. For you once were not a people, but now you are the people of God; you had not received mercy, but now you have received mercy" (1 Peter 2:9-10). We were created in God's image with intellectual abilities, the capacity to communicate, the ability to procreate, the freedom to make choices, a knowledge of right and wrong, and the responsibility to administer and rule over the rest of creation.

In his book *I Give You Authority*, Dr. Charles Kraft addresses two fascinating concepts regarding our status and connection with God. He discusses our position in creation, and he talks about the fact that we were made in God's image. The following is an adaptation of his view.

> *The Bible presents us with a very different view of who we are. When God created us, he positioned us a little lower than Himself. Thus Satan is jealous and angry. He especially attacks those who possess the things he cannot have such as creativity-the ability to procreate. He is envious of the position God has given us, i.e., just a bit lower than God Himself. "For you made us only a little lower than God, and you crowned us with glory and honor" (Psalm 8:5, NLT).*
>
> *In Genesis it says, " Let us make man in our image, in our likeness"(1:26). So Adam was made in the image of God, and although that image has been marred by sin we can still say that we are made in His image and have been given the privilege by God to procreate others in his image.*

> *Not only are we in the image of God, but God's "seed" is in us. "No one who is born of God will continue to sin, because God's seed remains in him; he cannot go on sinning because he has been born of God" (1 John 3:9).*
>
> *DNA has become a familiar term to us. Your DNA makes you different from everybody else. Your offspring have DNA that comes from you. They do not have to try to look like you, for since they have your DNA they will resemble you. If you have received God's seed (DNA) it will cause you to become more like Him. When you received Jesus Christ into your life as Lord, you received the Holy Spirit. You received God. In time, transformation will begin in your life because God is "Immanuel," God with us, and "For those God foreknew he also predestined to be conformed to the likeness of his Son, that He might be the firstborn among many brothers" (Romans 8:29).[4]*

In addition to these factors, God also made man to rule over the rest of His creation. "And let them rule over the fish of the sea and the birds of the air, over the livestock, over all the earth and over all the creatures that move along the ground. So God created man in his own image, in the image of God he created him; male and female he created them" (Genesis 1:26,27). " You put us in charge of everything you made, giving us authority over all things, the sheep and the cattle and all the wild animals, the birds in the sky, the fish in the sea, and everything that swims the ocean currents" (Psalms 8:6-8, NLT).

So we are made in God's image, we are positioned just below God, and we have been placed in this position to rule over all of creation. If these were not affirming enough in regard to our value, let us look at the book of Jeremiah: "Before I formed you in the womb I knew you"(Jeremiah1:5). God absolutely does not make mistakes. He formed you, and He likes what He formed!

The Catholic priest George Maloney writes about our uniqueness in his book *Alone with the Alone*. In the section entitled "The Gift of Yourself" he says,

"We do tend to take ourselves for granted. Reflect: There was a time when you did not exist, but there will never be another time when you will not exist. Yet in the mind of God, in His love for you, you always existed, for He had an idea in His mind that was you from all eternity. There was never a time when God was not thinking of you. He cannot love you more tomorrow than He loves you today and has loved you yesterday. Of all the billions of creatures possible that never saw the light of existence, you were chosen by God to be, to exist. And when in time He brought you forth, when on that certain day you became a human being, when this divine thought of God became incarnated in you, you were destined by God to go on living with His own eternity. You are never to cease to exist. What gratitude should there be for the gift of existence that makes your life so uniquely full of meaning, God-meaning, compared to other creatures destined by God only to be an aid for you to attain eternal life? Ponder prayerfully all the gifts of God wrapped up in your creation: your faculties of intellect, will, imagination, memory; your senses, so marvelous, so intricate and mysterious. You are made in God's image and likeness through your ability to think, know and love."[5]

Do you think God would have sent His only Son to die for us if we were not special? Not only did He send His Son, but He also sent angels to guard us, the Holy Spirit to guide us and the Scriptures to teach us. We are valuable enough to Him that we will spend eternity with Him in a place prepared for us in heaven. "Do not let your hearts be troubled. Trust in God; trust also in Me. In My Father's house are many rooms; if it were not so, I would have told you. I am going there to prepare a place for you. And if I go and prepare a place for you, I will come back and take you to be with Me that you also may be where I am. You know the way to the place where I am going" (Matthew 14:1).

Even with these promises we may yet think of God as being absent and uninvolved, so that in reality, we are left in a vast universe, fending for ourselves.

"But for all our fears we are not alone. Our trouble is that we think of ourselves as being alone. Let us correct the error by thinking of ourselves as standing by the bank of a full flowing river; then let us think of that river as being none else but God Himself. We glance to our left and see the river coming full out of our past; we look to the right and see it flowing on into our future. But we see also that it is flowing through our present. And in our today it is the same as it was in our yesterday, not less than, nor different from, but the very same river, one unbroken continuum, undiminished, active and strong as it moves sovereignly on into our tomorrow."[6]

Or in our woundedness and low self-esteem we perhaps think, "What about all the wrongs I have done, or the thoughts that I have?" We all sin, and sin leads to conflict with ourselves, others and God. Sin influences the way we feel about ourselves and often produces guilt that keeps us from God. But more than this, God loves us and values us. He knows we are ungodly and helpless, but that does not mean we are unredeemable and worthless. Because of His love and mercy He has brought us into His family as fully forgiven sons and daughters. While we understand that sin hinders relationship with God, in God's sight we are still at the apex of divine creation and of immense worth and value.

Are we supposed to feel good about ourselves then, to actually love ourselves? That is what Scripture says in numerous places. Why is it so difficult for us to accept this?

We Misunderstand Love

One of the biggest stumbling blocks we have in loving ourselves is our misunderstanding of love. At some point in life perhaps you have been taught that loving yourself was a form of pride. Scripture says, "Love your neighbor as you love yourself." A healthy love for yourself is not prideful. Pride is an arrogant estimation of one's self. Pride was Adam and Eve's sin and is the most dangerous of attitudes. That is not what Scripture says. Rather, Scriptures teaches us to love ourselves and that we are worthwhile creatures, valued and loved by God, gifted members of the Body of Christ and bearers of the Divine Image. Loving ourselves is a grateful dependence on God and a realistic appraisal of both our strengths and weaknesses.

The humble person acknowledges his imperfections, sins and failures but also acknowledges the gifts, abilities and achievements that come from God. Humility is not the rejection of our God-given strengths and abilities. We must understand that God loves us and has made us as He desired. We can acknowledge and accept our abilities, gifts and achievements because these come from God. We can experience the forgiveness of sins because God forgives unconditionally, and we can praise God for what He does in and through us. Thomas Kempis said, "A humble knowledge of one's self is a surer road to God than a deep searching of the sciences."[7]

Our sense of value and worth comes when we realize we are loved by God, who accepts us as we are, forgives our sins and makes us into new creatures. We become a whole person only when we stand with God.

I read an illustration entitled *The Candle*, source unknown: "The candle is like you and me. It has all it takes to be a candle-wax, wick, shape, color, odor-but it lacks something that alone will make it truly what it is. It needs a spark from outside itself, a gift of flame. Then it will give off light and warmth. Then it will be what it is meant to be. We are like that. We have all it takes to be human beings. Yet we need a gift, a spark of love from our God. Then we glow. Then we become warm and give off light. Before that we are as incomplete as the unlighted candle."

A popular teaching of the 1800s continually focused on the sinfulness of man. It portrayed us as needing to grovel before God about how bad and unworthy we were, begging Him to have mercy on us, even though we were too wretched to be in His presence. Satan would have us view God in such a way-as a harsh, imposing figure who waits to spoil all our fun. Satan encourages teaching that emphasizes our worthlessness, inadequacy and wretchedness and minimizes God's love, mercy and grace.

In 1 John 1:9 we are told that God freely forgives all who confess their sins. Now I am not making light of our sinfulness. I know that we can be in His presence only because of the cleansing blood of Jesus. But God, like a loving father, wants an intimate relationship with us. He wants us to come before Him so He can forgive us and we can have a deep sense and understanding of His love for us. I certainly do not want us to take lightly the privilege we have to appear before our Father God. Obviously there are times when we need to understand in whose presence we stand and when we need to enter into His presence with reverence and humility. But there are also times when we go into His presence dancing and singing, and there are times when we can rest in His arms of love.

RESULTS OF A POOR SELF-IMAGE

Even when we can begin to understand the fullness of God's love, a poor self-image can affect us in many ways.

A Lack of Trust

One of the most obvious is that we develop an inability to trust God. If you had said to me twenty-five years ago that someday I would be traveling around the world, praying for people, teaching leaders and participating in street evangelism in Eastern Europe, I would have responded, "No Way!" Why? One: I had no interest in doing this. Two: I was not sure I could trust God. I do not know the source for this story but it illustrates well a lack of trust.

> *A father was trying to teach his little boy, who was afraid of the dark, to trust God. One night his father told him to go out to the back porch and bring him a bucket. The little boy turned to his father and said, "Daddy, I do not want to go out there. It's dark." The father smiled reassuringly at his son and said, "You do not have to be afraid of the dark,*

for Jesus is out there. He will look after you and protect you." The little boy looked at his father and asked, "Are you sure He's out there?" "Yes, I am sure. He is everywhere, and He is always ready to help you when you need Him," he said. The little boy thought about that for a minute and then went to the back door, cracked it a little and, peering out into the darkness, called, "Jesus? If you're out there, would you please hand me the bucket?"

Perhaps this reminds you of your own fears. You want to trust God, but you do not seem able to stir up enough faith to do so. This is often a result of a deep rejection of self. You may know that God, who created everything-including you-is also all-wise and infinitely loving. But, you may think, if what you see in the mirror is an example of His creativity and His love, you may not be very impressed. When you look at the self whose image you despise, how can you believe He loves you, and how can you trust Him? This response overlooks what God is preparing to accomplish in and through our lives.

Rebellion

When we reject the self that God created, we begin to feel we have been cheated in life. Consciously or unconsciously we can develop the attitude that God owes us something. We see Him as an authority figure who has wronged us. So when another authority figure comes along laying down further restrictions that we feel will hinder our enjoyment of life even more, we are apt to resent this authority. Much of our rebellion is rooted in this rejection of self.

Inability to Build Genuine Relationships

This same self-rejection hinders both our responses to others and their responses to us. When we are oversensitive to the response others have to our appearance or abilities, we become unable to concentrate on their real needs. Thus, our ability to build genuine relationships is severely limited.

Seeking Acceptance and Approval

People who cannot accept themselves are apt to believe that others will not accept them either-that is, unless they do something to win their approval. They feel people will never care about them unless they do or become something significant. We compensate for our deficiencies by trying to achieve goals that will bring acceptance and approval from others, even if they have nothing to do with what we want to be or do in life. This desire for approval diverts our attention from the purpose and achievement God designed for us.

For example, growing up I wanted to be rich, have a respected position, the power that goes with that position and lots of material things! I felt those things were what I needed in order to be of value, to be somebody whom people respected. Interestingly enough, God put me in a position where I had most of what I wanted but then revealed to me how truly empty all that stuff that I thought was so important actually was.

Overemphasizing clothes, appearance or possessions is a normal reaction in those trying to cover up or detract attention from a rejection of self. While not all well-dressed people have a self-image problem, many are really saying, "Do not look at me-look at my stuff!"

Seeking acceptance and approval can take a number of forms. For example, people who as children never experienced parental love for who they truly were but, rather, only for what they accomplished, can become adults who are driven, insecure and critical. If a child hears praise focused solely on performance rather than personhood-such as, "Mommy loves Susie when she cleans up all her toys"-that child might view him or herself not as a human being but as a human "doing."

Others seeking approval might develop a Messiah Complex, i.e., an unrelenting serving of God through incredible amounts of activity such as going to church every time the doors are open; worshiping, praying, tithing, visiting the sick, etc. In other words, doing everything one possibly can do to receive approval from God. We pastors are especially vulnerable to this one. We feel we must help God out and expend incredible amounts of time and energy saving the world, often at the expense of our families and our health. Some people do whatever it takes to get noticed, even developing a habit of being bad. Such people have a way of doing things to provoke people to anger. Since their low self-esteem keeps them from seeking positive attention, they settle for negative attention. Such unhappy souls are often negative and critical of anyone who has achieved. Almost everything they try fails. They see themselves as losers, they act like losers, and as a result they usually turn out to be losers.

Negative Body or Mind Image

When we reject ourselves we typically have negative feelings toward our bodies or minds. For example, we typically reject our bodies or parts of our bodies that do not line up with what the media suggests we should have? Do you know many people with that type of body? That's my point! Rarely are the cultural standards for the size and shape of our bodies ever attained. Furthermore, we often see ourselves as not smart enough or overly emotional, and thus we are constantly directing negative thoughts and words toward ourselves.

When we move into a place of intimacy with Father God, we soon understand what it means to love ourselves. If I love myself, I am going to take care of and nurture myself-body, soul and spirit. That kind of nurture must come from relationship with my Creator, who helps me see myself as He sees me.

A Sense of Shame

Many have a sense of shame for even existing. It could come from a mother who was ashamed to be pregnant. I prayed once with a man whose mother became pregnant with him before she was married. He has dealt with issues of shame and blame for years. Trying to please others and gain approval from his mother drove him. Most shame-based people feel shame when they need help, when they feel angry, sad, fearful or joyous, or when they are sexually assertive.

Shame also can come from one's own name. When I was growing up I disliked my name, Michael, for this is what my mother always called me when I was in trouble. I wanted to be called Mike, especially when I entered junior high school. For some reason *Michael* seemed weak, and *Mike* seemed stronger and more masculine. Later, when I began to understand who I was in Christ and that Michael is one of the most powerful Warrior Angels in the Bible, I was no longer ashamed and decided it was okay to be called *Michael*.

In his book *Healing the Shame that Binds You*, John Bradshaw talks about toxic shame, suggesting that it is the core and fuel of all addiction. We are looking for ways to deal with the shame. We may use alcohol, drugs, sex or some other behavior to cover the shame. He even suggests that some, who at the deepest level do not like themselves, may use religion to cover shame just as an addict uses drugs. He makes a rather startling statement regarding such religious behavior.

> *"Religious addiction is rooted in toxic shame, which can be readily mood- altered through various religious behaviors. One can get feelings of righteousness through any form of worship. One can fast, pray, meditate, serve others, go through sacramental rituals, speak in tongues, be slain by the Holy Spirit, quote the Bible, read Bible passages, say the name of Yahweh or Jesus. Any of these can be mood-altering experiences."[8]*

Such use of religion to cover shame may be rooted in an incorrect image of sin and grace. We are indeed sinners. We commit sins. But when we confess, God forgives those sins and they are erased. We do not have to feel shame or continually focus on our sinfulness. "No one who is born of

God will continue to sin, because God's seed remains in him; he cannot go on sinning, because he has been born of God" (1 John 3:9). It is enough to commit to God anything we may have done, knowingly or unknowingly, and to recognize that he forgives it as soon as we confess it. We are no longer sinners-we are saints!

Cursing Ourselves

Sometimes people say hateful things about themselves. In his book *I Give You Authority*, Dr. Charles Kraft tells the story of a woman who came for prayer because of lumps on her breasts. The Lord revealed to Dr. Kraft that she had put a curse on her breasts. She confessed that she had been abused as a teenager, and the abuse focused on her breasts. Dr. Kraft had her pray, "In the name of Jesus, I renounce any curse I have put on myself." Almost immediately the lumps on her breasts went away.[9]

WE ARE AT WAR!

A poor self-image and all of the accompanying beliefs are simply lies! Satan uses whatever means he has available to defeat or destroy us, attacking our self-esteem, abilities, gifts, achievements and failures. He uses feelings of shame, abandonment and rejection to keep us in bondage. Anything he can do to keep us from understanding our value and identity as the Beloved of God, he will do.

We must recognize that we are at war. We are in battle "against the spiritual forces of evil in the heavenly realms" (Ephesians 6:12). He is trying to take us down. He uses family members, good friends, Christians-anyone we love and trust. He attacks us with abusive words, accusations and condemnation. He takes any opportunity to influence people around us to hurt us or even destroy us.

In my travels, I am amazed to find a great number of people who do not have a clue that they are in a war. Some say, "We do not need to spend time focused on Satan and his schemes; we just need to know God." Many think that if they ignore him he will go away. While we must not spend a great deal of time focused on Satan, neither should we ignore him. John Maxwell said, "No good general goes into battle without a thorough understanding of the enemy. To do so is presumptuous and stupid." We need to know that the enemy is always on the prowl to destroy us.

FIGHTING THE BATTLE

Claim Protection

We need to consistently claim the protection that is ours in Christ. Unless sent as an ambassador of Christ, stop going places where your worth and value are constantly attacked. As far as possible, stop hanging around people who are always negative, and stop associating unnecessarily with people who wound you. Stop entertaining negative self-perceptions like: "I am no good. I am a loser. I'll never be able to do anything right."

Know Who You Are in Christ

Instead, understand what the Scripture says about who we are in Christ. None of us is a mistake! Conception is not simply a physical, human act. Only God can give the life that courses through our physical bodies. He was not surprised at our conception but affirmed it by granting us life. Since we were not accidents, we must never allow anyone to convince us that we are mistakes!

Why is it so important for us to know these truths-truths that reveal God's heart for us? It is crucial for our survival! In his book, *The Bondage Breaker*, Neil Anderson breaks it down this way:

> *You Are Accepted/You are God's child. "Yet to all who received Him, to those who believed in His name, he gave the right to become children of God" (John 1:12).*

> *You Are Secure/You cannot be separated from the love of God. "Who shall separate us from the love of Christ? Shall*

trouble or hardship or persecution or famine or nakedness or danger or sword?" (Romans 8:35).

You are Significant/You are God's workmanship. "For we are God's workmanship, created in Christ Jesus to do good works, which God prepared in advance for us to do" (Ephesians 2:10).[10]

Do Not Focus on Circumstances

We often focus on circumstances, but circumstances are not meant to affect us as much as they generally do. Sometimes our circumstances seem overwhelming and we are apt to think that they control us. We may think that because we were born into a poor family we will always be poor, or we will never be very intelligent because our parents did not have a high IQ. If we were treated poorly or verbally abused we may feel as if we are of little value.

Neil Anderson says in his book *Victory Over The Darkness*:

"No person can consistently behave in a way that's inconsistent with the way he perceives himself. If you think you're a no-good bum, you'll probably live like a no-good bum. But if you see yourself as a child of God who is spiritually alive in Christ, you'll begin to live in victory and freedom as He lived. Next to a knowledge of God, a knowledge of who you are is by far the most important truth you can possess...Self-worth is not an issue of giftedness, talent, intelligence or beauty. Self-worth is an identity issue. Your sense of personal worth comes from knowing who you are: a child of God."[11]

Furthermore, history proves that you can rise above circumstances. I have never forgotten a paragraph I read in John Maxwell's book, *Developing The Leader Within You*:

"Many great people began life in the poorest and most humble of homes, with little education and no advantages. Thomas Edison was a newsboy on trains. Andrew Carnegie started work at four dollars a month, and John D. Rockefeller

at six dollars a week. The remarkable thing about Abraham Lincoln was not that he was born in a log cabin, but that he got out of the log cabin. Demosthenes, the greatest orator of the ancient world, stuttered! The first time he tried to make a public speech, he was laughed off the rostrum. Julius Caesar was an epileptic. Napoleon was of humble parentage and far from a born genius-he stood forty-sixth in his class at the military academy in a class of sixty-five). Beethoven was deaf, as was Thomas Edison. Charles Dickens was lame; so was Handel. Homer was blind; Plato was a hunchback; Sir Walter Scott was paralyzed."[12]

Renew Your Mind

The Scriptures teach us to renew our minds. What does this mean, and how do we do it? Renewal of one's mind involves pulling down strongholds and fortresses of thought patterns and bringing each thought into captivity to Christ. "The weapons we fight with are not the weapons of the world. On the contrary, they have divine power to demolish strongholds. We demolish arguments and every pretension that sets itself up against the knowledge of God, and we take captive every thought to make it obedient to Christ" (2Corinthians 10:4-5).

Thoughts that set themselves up against the knowledge of God must be replaced with biblically based thoughts. We must learn to think God's truth, focusing on "whatever is true, whatever is honorable, whatever is right, whatever is pure, whatever is lovely, whatever is of good repute" (Philippians.4:8).

Believers are commanded to renew their minds because temptations originate in one's thoughts. "Do not conform any longer to the pattern of this world, but be transformed by the renewing of your mind" (Romans 12:2). "You have heard that it was said, do not commit adultery. But I tell you that anyone who looks at a woman lustfully has already committed adultery with her in his heart" (Matthew 5:27-28).

Scripture teaches us that Satan is the father of all lies and, consequently, the mind is his chief battleground. Believers are, therefore, instructed to put on the full armor of God to fight the enemy (Ephesians 6:10-18). Three elements of this armor are vital to the protection of one's thought life: the belt of truth, the helmet of salvation and the sword of the Spirit, which is the Word of God. They provide the controlling influence on one's emotions and will. All these are to be covered with prayer.

Renewal of one's thought life is essential to victorious Christian living. Believers have been given the mind of Christ. "For who has known the mind of the Lord that He may instruct him? But we have the mind of Christ" (1 Corinthians 2:16). Therefore, we must agree with God's thoughts rather than the enemy's lies.

Wait in Silence

In Psalm 62, verse 1 reads, "My soul waits in silence for God only." This verse is better translated, "Only for God in silence does my soul wait." The word "silence" comes from the Hebrew word that means "to whisper softly." It conveys the idea of whispering a secret to somebody you love, but not loud enough for anyone else to hear. In verse 5, David again commands his soul to be still and to "wait in silence for God only." He is talking to his soul and commanding it to be still.

You know how difficult it is to be still and quietly concentrate on the Lord. When you try this, your mind becomes occupied with all the things you think you should be doing. Many distracting thoughts come ripping through your mind. While some of them are priority matters that must be attended to immediately, others can wait. For example, after not ringing all day, the telephone will come to life. To be still and wait quietly is a challenge in our fast paced, instant communication, instant food culture. But waiting in silence is required in order to nurture our relationship with Him.

A Nurturing Relationship

Because of many of the factors mentioned in this chapter, many of us lack a nurturing relationship with God. Such a relationship allows us to speak and act from strength rather than from fear or insecurity. Only in a true nurturing relationship with Him can we understand our true value and worth. Most importantly, a nurturing relationship with the Father helps us to be comfortable sitting quietly in His presence.

I again raise the questions I asked at the beginning of this chapter. Do you really want to live every moment of your life in His presence? Do you want to long for Him, to thirst for Him? Do you want to hunger to be in His presence? "Do you want to live in such an amazing divine Presence that life is transformed and transfigured and transmuted into peace and power and glory and miracle?"[13]

Do you want your soul to pant for Him?

If you want to love God above all else in the world-with all your heart, soul, mind and strength (Mark 12:30)- you must nurture your relationship with Him. And in order to do so, an intimate relationship with God must become so important that it stirs a fire within our inmost being-a fire burning out all excuses, all false humility, all shallowness, all dishonesty and all those hindrances to which we have clung and behind which we feel so safe. Only then can we establish an intimate relationship with Him. And only in an intimate relationship with Him can our souls truly be nurtured.

3

THE BENEFITS OF WAITING ON GOD

I t is a difficult thing for us to be still and wait. I said earlier that we are an impatient people. We are used to taking control and making things happen. If something is not going as well as we think it should, we take action to change it. It is quite normal for us to make plans and then pray for God to give us counsel and to bless our plans. All too soon, we begin to implement what we have just finished praying about without waiting for an answer. We are used to going ahead and doing things, rather than waiting for God to lead us. But when we sit still and wait upon God, He will direct, protect and correct us.

Scripture Teaches Us to Wait Upon God

In Samuel 10:7-8, Saul had just been anointed king by the prophet Samuel and was instructed by the prophet to do nothing independently of him. Samuel had told Saul to go down to Gilgal where Samuel would join him after seven days and offer burnt offerings and sacrifice peace offerings.

Three years passed before Saul actually traveled to Gilgal. In 1 Samuel 13, the people of Israel, who had joined Saul in Gilgal, found themselves facing an overwhelming army of Philistines. The situation was so critical that their army, "hid in caves and thickets, among the rocks, and in pits and cisterns" (verse 6).

"Saul remained at Gilgal, and all the troops with him were quaking with fear. He waited seven days, the time set by Samuel; but Samuel did not come to Gilgal, and Saul's men began to scatter. So he said, 'Bring me the burnt offering and the fellowship offerings'" (1 Samuel 13:7-8). Saul and his army had journeyed to Gilgal and waited for seven days as Samuel had instructed him. After the seven days the troops became restless. Rather than waiting on Samuel, Saul took matters into his own hands and offered a burnt offering to unite the people and prepare for war. "Just as he finished making the offering, Samuel arrived, and Saul went out to greet him" (verse 10).

Rather than confessing his sin, Saul tried to excuse his actions and justify himself. "Well, the troops were getting restless, and you did not come when you said you would, so I had no choice." He thought he simply could not wait. He was impatient, and he was afraid of his men. Consequently, he did something rash and took matters into his own hands. Samuel was upset with Saul and informed him that because of his disobedience his kingdom would not last.

Samuel's words may seem a bit harsh, but he had made it clear to Saul that God was looking for a man after his own heart. He wanted a man who would obey without fear or question, who would wait upon the Lord and trust Him as his provider.

Scripture Teaches that God is Our Provider

Scripture contains numerous illustrations describing God as a provider. For example, the book of Exodus shows how God provided food and water in the desert for His people, a way of escape from Pharoah across the Red Sea, a cloud to protect them by day and a fire to guide them by night.

Remember when the people of Israel were out in the desert, camping at a place where there was no water? They began to grumble and murmur against Moses (Exodus 17:1-7). He cried out to God, "What am I supposed to do with these people? They are ready to kill me" (verse 4). God told Moses to gather some of the elders and to strike a rock at Horeb where water would come out. He did as instructed, and water gushed out from the rock! In reading the story of God's dealing with Israel in Exodus, it is obvious that again and again He was trying to reveal to them that He could provide whatever they needed.

We scurry around frantically taking care of and worrying about things God can easily handle. We do this because we do not think we should bother God with such small things, or we do not believe He is concerned about the details in our lives. Or perhaps we have been taught that God helps those who help themselves. Or maybe it is simply that we do not know or understand all the ways He is willing to provide. Someone wrote,

> *Said the Robin to the Sparrow, "I would really like to know*
> *Why these anxious human beings rush about and worry*
> *so."*
> *Said the Sparrow to the Robin, "Friend, I think that it must*
> *be*
> *That they have no Heavenly Father such as cares for you*
> *and me." (source unknown)*

God is aware that we must have food, clothing and shelter to survive. He says He will provide these things if we seek His Kingdom. "And why do you worry about clothes? See how the lilies of the field grow. They do not labor or spin. Yet I tell you that not even Solomon in all his splendor was dressed like one of these. If that is how God clothes the grass of the field, which is here today and tomorrow is thrown into the fire, will he not much more clothe you, O you of little faith? So do not worry, saying, 'What shall we eat?' or 'What shall we drink?' or 'What shall we wear?' For the pagans run after all these things and your heavenly Father knows that you need them. But seek first his kingdom and his righteousness, and all these things will be given to you as well. Therefore do not worry about tomorrow, for tomorrow will worry about itself. Each day has enough trouble of its own" (Matthew.6:28-34).

We sometimes lightly say to others, "Just trust in God. He will provide." But as we go about our everyday lives, our actions do not often indicate we believe that He will indeed provide. As long as we have job security, money for the bills and maybe a little in the bank, we are content and find it easy to say, "Life is good. I am trusting God. He is providing." But if something in this picture radically shifts, our first response is often, "God, why did you let this happen to me?" or "God, what did I do wrong?"

It is somewhat comforting to realize this is a normal reaction of men and women throughout the Scriptures. In Psalm 21, David rejoices in all God has given him-his victories, rich blessings, a crown on his head, splendor, majesty and eternal blessings. But just a bit later in Psalm 22 he cries out, "My God, my God, why have you forsaken me? Why are you so far from saving me, so far from the words of my groaning?" (verse 1). There is not much difference between how they reacted and how we react.

God's Provision for Abraham

Genesis 22:1-13 tells how God called Abraham to sacrifice his son, Isaac. We do not usually think of this as an example of God providing. Rather, when we look at this story we see it as an example of the faith of Abraham, a faith that brought him to a point of being willing to sacrifice his own son. But beyond the lesson of faith, we must recognize that God provided for Abraham in the midst of this trial.

In this passage it says God tested Abraham. He did not tempt him, for God does not tempt. But He does test to confirm our faith and prove our commitment. Abraham's immediate response was that of a trusting servant: "Here I am."

God said to Abraham, "I want your only son, whom you love." God is not asking Abraham to do a small thing-this is the son of the promise! It sounds rather cold and matter of fact. If I were in Abraham's position, I would probably have responded: "God, you want me to take my only son, tie him to an altar and kill him in sacrifice to you? You must be joking! I asked for this son, and you provided him after many years, and now you want me to kill him? What kind of a God are you? Surely you do not understand what you're asking me to do!"

Abraham had committed himself by covenant to be obedient to the Lord and had consecrated his son Isaac to the Lord by the act of circumcision. So God put his faith and loyalty to the test. It is interesting that Abraham responded promptly- "early the next morning" (verse 3). I suspect that just like us, he spent a long night in turmoil and prayer with God. "God, are you sure? You really want me to do this?" And he did it. Not after a week or a month, but the next morning.

And Abraham did not just go outside his tent and do this sacrifice at the local altar. He had to travel three days to Mt. Moriah. Can you imagine what those three days were like for him, as he and his son walked along together, as they laughed and talked and slept and ate? Do you imagine his son was excited to be going with his father? What a heavy burden this was for his father to bear.

Genesis 22:7-8 makes it sound so matter of fact! "Isaac spoke up and said to his father Abraham, 'Father?' 'Yes, my son?' Abraham replied. 'The fire and wood are here,' Isaac said, 'but where is the lamb for the burnt offering?' Abraham answered, 'God himself will provide the lamb for the burnt offering, my son."

Imagine what Isaac must have been thinking. "Here I am carrying this heavy load of wood up this mountain. We've got to climb all the way to the top, and there isn't a lamb around here for 200 miles."

Better still, imagine what must have gone on between Abraham and Isaac as the father tied up his son and laid him on the altar. Did you ever wonder how he was able to accomplish this? Isaac was not a little kid. Most likely, he was a boy of about 15 and probably quite strong and healthy from working among his father's flocks and fields. Do you think Isaac just quietly and passively lay there? I think he was scared and knew as he was lying there what his father was planning to do. He must have thought, "I know for sure he has lost it. He is going to kill me, his favorite son!" And from Abraham's point of view, it must have been quite unsettling to stand poised with this knife in his hand, ready to plunge it into Isaac.

Abraham was at the most desperate, lowest point of his life, brought about as a result of his covenant and obedience to God. He knew what God was asking him to do, but he also knew and trusted that somehow God would bring his son back to him. He did not know how, and he did not know why God was asking him to do this thing. He did not understand, and I am sure he did not like it. But the important point is that he did it! Only then did God stop him and provide a lamb for the sacrifice.

Will God, as our provider, do any less for us if we are willing to totally give all we have and all we are to Him? If we allow Him, God will provide for our needs.

Our Needs Are No Surprise to God

We constantly question God, asking, "How are you going to do this?" or "When are you going to do this?" We ask these questions as if it has not occurred to Him what we need. Did it ever occur to you that nothing "occurs" to God? Do you think your needs ever surprise Him? It does not take a high IQ to figure out that He knows what we need. Matthew 6:28-34 makes it clear that He is aware of our needs.

Over seven years ago, God told me to trust Him for everything. I was sitting by a river near my home and we were having a conversation about my future. At one point I asked him, "God, are you saying you want me to resign from my position with the church, giving up my salary and security?" He said, "Yes, you can no longer do there what I want you to do." I said, "But God, you do not understand. I have kids, house payment, bills, etc." He said, "What's the problem?" I replied, "WHAT'S THE PROBLEM! What about the bills, food, etc.?" He interrupted me and said, "Michael, what's the problem?"

Suddenly the lights came on and I realized that I was, after all, talking to God! So what's the problem? God was saying to me, "Michael, I know what your needs are. I am asking you to do something you've never done before. Are you going to trust Me?"

MY OWN JOURNEY OF FAITH IN MY PROVIDER

But even before this encounter with God seven years ago, my journey of faith in my Provider had begun. Wholeness Ministries was founded in 1989. Our purpose is to pray for healing and to train and equip others to pray for healing. We offer training at our offices in California and conduct conferences and workshops both nationally and internationally. The majority of our support comes by donation from a group of faithful supporters. It is easy to talk about faith and trust and to walk in it for short periods of time. But over the long haul God begins to dig deep into our very souls and expose those areas of our lives that want to be in control.

About the middle of the year 2000, I hit the wall! I was discouraged and beat down. I was tired of listening to people, praying for people, worrying about finances, returning phone calls, writing newsletters and handling the numerous administrative details of ministry. I had no emotional or physical strength to change anything, nor did I even want to change it. I was burned out and depressed.

Personally, I had never dealt with this level of depression before. I wanted to be left alone. One day my wife, Jane, handed me a book written about burnout. I did not recognize what was happening to me, but as I read the book I realized how closely I fit the profile of one in burnout. It was difficult to admit that I was burned out. At the insistence of my wife, I took a sabbatical to allow my body, emotions and spirit a time of rest and restoration.

During this time I began to examine and deal with some things about myself that I did not want to face. They were issues that only I knew were there. These places were ugly and deeply rooted in the flesh, places where I worried over the finances, or over what was not happening, or things I thought I could fix.

When you are depressed the last thing you want to hear is people telling you all the wonderful things God is going to pour out on you if you will just be patient and trust Him. You do not want to be told to have a happy heart because your strength and joy is from the Lord. This just further frustrates and depresses you. Proverbs says it best. "Like one who takes off a garment on a cold day, or like vinegar on soda, is he who sings songs to a troubled heart" (Proverbs 25:20). When you are in depression, you want to know if not now, when? How long do I have to wait for this?

At the deepest point of my despair, what I wanted to say back to people was, "Give me a break! I am sick of hearing these trite religious clichés dribble from your mouth. You do not have a clue what I am going through, and frankly I do not know that God even cares because He is obviously not doing anything to help or I would not be in this mess!"

During this time in my life I had to deal with my own trust in God, faith in God, and even my blatant and childish ungratefulness for what God had done in the past and was doing in the present. That's a sobering place to be.

WE ARE OFTEN UNGRATEFUL

Lest you think my reaction was unique, Scripture is full of examples of ungratefulness for God's provision. For example, even after all God had done for them, the Israelites still were not satisfied. In Numbers we read, "The rabble with them began to crave other food, and again the Israelites started wailing and said, "If only we had meat to eat! We remember the fish we ate in Egypt at no cost-also the cucumbers, melons, leeks, onions and garlic. But now we have lost our appetite; we never see anything but this manna" (Numbers 11:4-6)!

They barely made it out of Egypt with their lives and had crossed the Red Sea via a miraculous work of God, and now they were wailing, complaining and murmuring about the manna God provided because they wanted meat. Remember that advertising slogan, "Where's the Beef?" That's what they were saying. We, like them, are at times demanding, spoiled, ungrateful children.

A little further in this same chapter (verses 10-15), "Moses heard the people of every family wailing, each at the entrance to his tent. The Lord became exceedingly angry, and Moses was troubled. He asked the Lord, 'Why have you brought this trouble on your servant? What have I done to displease You that You put the burden of all these people on me? Did I conceive all these people? Did I give them birth? Why do You tell me to carry them in my arms, as a nurse carries an infant, to the land you promised on oath to their forefathers? Where can I get meat for all these people? They keep wailing to me, "Give us meat to eat!" I cannot carry all these people by myself; the burden is too heavy for me. If this is how you are going to treat me, put me to death right now-if I have found favor in your eyes-and do not let me face my own ruin.'" Imagine Moses reaching the point where he told God, "I have had enough! I want out! What have I done to deserve this? Just put me to death!"

God responded by saying, "Tell the people: 'Consecrate yourselves in preparation for tomorrow, when you will eat meat. The Lord heard you when you wailed, "If only we had meat to eat! We were better off in Egypt!" Now the Lord will give you meat, and you will eat it. You will not eat it for just one day, or two days, or five, ten or twenty days, but for a whole month-until it comes out of your nostrils and you loathe it-because you have rejected the Lord, who is among you, and have wailed before him, saying, "Why did we ever leave Egypt?"'" (Numbers 11:18-20).

Basically what He was saying to them was, "You want meat? I'll give you meat!" The Lord caused a wind that brought in quail from the sea, and they fell all around the camp to about three feet above the ground, as far as a day's walk in any direction (verse 31). Assume you can walk about twenty miles in a day. So, in every direction you look, extending out for twenty miles, you see quail piled three feet deep! That was the result of their murmuring and complaining. Do you think this can be described as childish ungratefulness?

We do not trust in God, and then we go one step farther and complain about what He does provide for us.

LEARNED TO WAIT

During this time in my life when I hit the wall, I literally could do nothing but wait for God. I was not walking in much faith or trust. I did not trust Him to provide and felt frustrated that the work I was doing was not producing any income to pay the bills. It is easy for us to say we trust God when needs are adequately being met, but it is hard to walk it out in faith when they're not.

God began teaching me this lesson when our book *Learning To Do What Jesus Did* was being translated into Hungarian. I received an e-mail that stated, "We are ready to print the book. In order to obtain the best price for the quantity of books we are printing we need another one thousand dollars, and we need it now." In frustration, I responded, "If I am going to send you another thousand dollars, God is going to have to drop it into my hands in the next 24 hours. Since I do not see that happening, go with what money you have and print as many as you can print!"

Early the next morning a man, obviously troubled, called and asked if he could come to the office and talk with me. He came to my office in tears. After a couple of hours of talking and praying together we finished, and he started to leave. Suddenly he stopped in the doorway, turned around, reached his hand into his back pocket, pulled out his wallet and said, "God told me to give you this." He proceeded to place in my hands ten brand new one hundred dollar bills. I started laughing at God's sense of humor. It had been less than twenty-four hours, and here was the money, dropped into my hands. I quickly sent an e-mail to my friends in Hungary: "I have the money. Go for the larger volume."

SILENCE AND STILLNESS EQUAL REST

When we come to realize that God is responsible for us and that He will provide, then we understand how important it is to "waste time with Him." Waiting in silence and stillness becomes healing to us. Our efforts, no matter how much of ourselves we expend, cannot produce the rest of God or the life of God within us. The only way that God's rest can be produced in us is when we come to Him to spend time with Him.

I love the song that says: "Father God, I am here to spend this time drawing near. I have not come to ask of you, I just want to be with you. To be with you in quiet and peace, to know the joy of sweet release, and face to face I know it's true, I just want to be with you."[1]

In his book *Holiness, Truth and the Presence of God*, Francis Frangipane writes, "What program, what degree of ministerial professionalism, can compare with the life and power we receive through Him?

Many leaders have worked themselves nearly to exhaustion seeking to serve God. If they spent half their time with Him, in prayer and waiting before Him, they would find His supernatural accompaniment working mightily in their efforts. They would become passengers in the vehicle of His will, a vehicle in which He Himself is both Captain and Navigator."[2]

Silence is defined as "The absence of sound; stillness. A period of time without speech or noise."[3] Scripture tells us, "There is a time for everything, and a season for every activity under heaven...a time to be silent and a time to speak" (Ecclesiastes 3:1,7). Richard Foster calls silence "a stilling of creaturely activity." He writes: "In prayer, we have become, as the early Church father Clement of Alexandria says, like old shoes—all worn out except for the tongue."[4]

It is difficult for us to be silent. We find silence uncomfortable. Our homes and cars are filled with a constant barrage of noise from our televisions, radios and stereos. One day while talking to a friend about backpacking, I said that what I enjoyed about backpacking was being up in the mountains away from all the noise. He responded, "I don't like backpacking." I asked, "Why not?" and he replied, "It's too quiet for me, makes me uneasy."

We have the distinction of being able to communicate more and say less than any civilization in history. Our answering machines save messages from people we do not want to hear from. Call waiting allows people with whom we do not want to talk to interrupt our phone conversations. In fact, we are so ingenious that we have invented phone systems enabling us to call anyone twenty-four hours a day. And after punching enough buttons on the phone to play the theme song from the Titanic, we can leave a message on the answering machine of the secretary of the secretary of the person to whom we wish to speak!

Brennan Manning says:

> *Silence is not simply the absence of noise or the shutdown of communication with the outside world, but rather a process of coming to stillness. Silent solitude forges true speech. I'm not speaking of physical isolation; solitude here means being alone with the Alone, experiencing the transcendent Other and growing in awareness of one's identity as the beloved. It is impossible to know another person intimately without spending time together. Silence makes this solitude a reality. It has been said, "Silence is solitude practiced in action."[5]*

Silence is especially difficult because it requires discipline. We do not necessarily like discipline, but without it we accomplish nothing. In *The Road Less Traveled*, Scott Peck says; "Without discipline we can solve nothing. With only some discipline we can solve only some problems. With total discipline we can solve all problems."[6]

Once we sit still in silence with Him we will know true peace and rest. He asks from us nothing but ourselves. He is not awed by our beautiful church buildings or our professional, programmed worship services. Not that these things are wrong when they are used for the purposes He intends. But He does not want what we have, nor does He want what we do. He wants us-unequivocally, unreservedly and without pretense. His desire is to create in us a place where He may come and abide, a place where our souls can find rest. God knows our rest is in Him.

In the Old Testament, the Sabbath was not a source of rest for God. It was a source of rest for man. Our rest, our growth, our renewal are found in God. Everything we really want to be and everything God wants to do in transforming and conforming us will be realized when we wait before Him. Fulfillment is found when we spend time with Him, allow Him to enfold us in his arms, crawl up into His lap and lay our head on his chest and cease our pitiful efforts for His approval. It is okay to cease striving for approval, acceptance or success. It is okay with God for us to just be ourselves, for He loves us and wants us to be with Him even though we are doing absolutely nothing but enjoying His Presence.

Some of my most intimate times of prayer are those quiet moments when I say absolutely nothing. This is usually early in the morning when it is quiet and before the busyness of the day starts. Now, I am not one of these who jumps up at four or five o'clock in the morning, ready to have my quiet time with God. At that time of the day I haven't had enough quiet time with myself! I am not awake enough to remember to whom it is I am talking, so it is ridiculous for me to tell you I am up before dawn, on my knees for three hours before I start my day. When I do get up, what I usually do is pour myself a cup of coffee, sit quietly in a comfortable chair and listen for God to speak to me.

This is a wonderful time because my mind is not yet busy with the tasks of the day. As I quietly wait, I do not hear an audible voice, but I sense what I believe God is saying. Sometimes He gives me a word or a sentence. Sometimes we carry on a conversation. Some of you may think this is a little ridiculous, but think about it. If we go before God and ask Him to speak to us, why are we so surprised when He actually does!

One of the early church fathers, Father Ammons, wrote, "I have shown you the power of silence, how thoroughly it heals and how fully pleasing it is to God...Know that it is by silence that the saints grew, that it was because of silence that the power of God dwelt in them, because of silence that the mysteries of God were known to them." [7]

When we wait quietly before God, not distracted by noise, it is generally true that we hear God's voice more clearly. This is important, as it is that very silence and stillness that not only contributes to our nurture but is healing to our souls and spirits. Not only do we have the benefit of Him as our provider, but also as our peace and rest.

4

ARE YOU LISTENING?

S pending significant time with God in solitude and silence is the only way we will develop and grow in deep intimacy with Him. Spending time with God will result in both understanding and living in the knowledge that we are accepted and loved as we are. We can come to Him in all our brokenness, and He will not withhold His love because of our brokenness and sin. As we embrace the brokenness and fully accept what we are, we allow Him to love us and heal us.

Meaningful, life-changing growth in this reflective lifestyle consists of two key elements. We have seen that the first is to sit in solitude and silence before Him. But we also must learn how to listen to Him. "Let the wise listen and add to their learning, and let the discerning get guidance" (Proverbs 1:5). "My sheep listen to my voice; I know them and they follow me" (John 10:27).

Prayer Involves Listening

The simplest definition of prayer is conversation with God. It involves both speaking and listening. James says, "Everyone should be quick to listen, slow to speak and slow to become angry" (James 1:19). So often we are quick to speak and slow to listen. In many ways we have lost the art of listening. While engaged in conversation with another, we may be only half-listening because we are thinking through what we will say in response when the person is finished speaking. Unfortunately, a good speaker is more highly regarded than a good listener.

In addition, though we may listen, often our agenda is much more important to us, so we listen to what we want to hear and ignore what does not fit with what we want. We often do this with God. We may receive an answer from Him, but because it does not correspond with what we want to do, we go back to Him to talk it over. Then, assuming we have His blessing, we move ahead, usually encountering opposition. This makes us angry, and we then blame God for the mess in which we find ourselves.

Balaam and His Donkey

The story of Balaam and his talking donkey (Numbers 22) is the perfect example of a man who did not like God's answer, went back to him to try to get a different one, and moved ahead, only to suffer the consequences. Balaam earned his living as a prophet and had a reputation as a man with the ability to cause significant things to happen when he spoke either blessings or curses. Balak, the king, summoned Balaam because he wanted him to curse the nation of Israel. But God said to Balaam, "You must not put a curse on those people, because they are blessed" (verse 12). So at first the prophet refused the king by saying, "The Lord has refused to let me go" (verse 13). But then he decided he would go back and ask again.

Why would Balaam go back and ask God again when he had already received a very clear answer to his prayer?

Possibly Balaam thought, "They have offered me a great deal of money to do this. I am going to go back and see if I can reason with God and perhaps change His mind." Balaam's desire was different from what God had told him to do, so Balaam wanted to go back and make a deal with God. He was trying to convince God to change His mind, and he was trying to justify his actions. Balaam was talking to God, but he was not listening to what God was saying.

Balaam persisted, and finally God relented and let him go. But "God was very angry when he went" (verse 22). God gave Balaam the answer he wanted. Balaam was so intent on his agenda that he was not going to let anything stop him. God knew what was in Balaam's heart, and He wanted to teach him through this situation that when God says no He means no.

God tried three different times to get Balaam's attention. He tried to divert him, brought physical pain and finally blocked his path. Balaam's response was to beat his donkey. Balaam was so spiritually blinded by his own pride and greed that he could not see that his opposition was coming from the Lord, rather than the donkey.

God could have chosen any number of ways to get Balaam's attention, but He used a donkey. That alone is hilarious in its absurdity. He had to resort to something so ridiculous that it made Balaam look foolish. Donkeys were not highly respected for their intelligence. They were viewed as dumb beasts of burden and were used for routine tasks. They were not noticed by anyone as long as they did their jobs and caused no trouble. It is obvious from this story that God will use any means necessary-even a donkey-to get our attention and attempt to stop us from doing something foolish. If God resorted to something this ridiculous to get your attention, would you listen?

This was a defining moment for Balaam. If he had simply obeyed in the first place, this entire incident could have been avoided.

Perhaps this is a defining moment for you. If you want relationship and intimacy with God, if you want to hear His voice, it is imperative that you wait, listen and obey.

Sometimes God lets us proceed with what we have determined to do, but that does not necessarily mean that He is pleased or will bless us in it. If we persist in going our own way, He will let us, but often He will bring opposition to try and turn us from our disobedience.

We learn from Balaam's experience that when we go to God to sit and listen, we must go with no agenda or preconceived ideas of what we expect to hear. If we determine to be with Him in solitude and silence, waiting expectantly to hear what He has to say to us, He will speak to us. When we sit quietly before God, He will purge our hearts with the fire of His love and truth. When we lay our requests before Him and listen to Him, His cleansing fire will reveal to us our motives, which could keep us from making costly mistakes.

DISCERNING THE VOICE OF GOD

As we wait before Him in solitude and silence, we also develop an intimacy in our relationship with Him that is much like that of which David speaks in Psalm 37: "Trust in the Lord and do good; dwell in the land and enjoy safe pasture. Delight yourself in the Lord and He will give you the desires of your heart. Commit your way to the Lord; trust in Him and He will do this; He will make your righteousness shine like the dawn, the justice of your cause like the noonday sun" (verses 3-6). His delight, trust and rest were in the Lord. Even a casual reading of the Psalms indicates David's relationship with God was intimate and strong. He is called a "man after God's own heart." Does this stem from David's perfection? It is obvious from Scripture that he was not perfect, but he longed to do God's will with all his heart. He wanted to hear from God and to develop an intimate, growing relationship with Him. God honored the desire of David's heart, and he grew in his discernment of God's voice.

Discernment is a vital tool in any type of ministry. It is a gift of the Holy Spirit and is given to us when we become believers. As with all the spiritual gifts, as we grow in the use of discernment we become more adept at recognizing the voice of God. "The man without the Spirit does not accept the things that come from the Spirit of God, for they are foolishness to him, and he cannot understand them, because they are spiritually discerned" (1 Corinthians 2:14). "But solid food is for the mature who by constant use have trained themselves to distinguish good from evil" (Hebrews. 5:14).

People often ask me, " How do you hear from God, and how do you know for sure that it is God speaking?" God does not normally speak to me in an audible voice, and seldom do I have dreams or see visions. Typically, when I am worshipping or praying, thoughts come into my mind that have significance for the person with whom I am praying or for someone else in the room who has a prayer need. I then speak the words audibly, they respond, and we pray for that specific need.

Early in my experience of learning how to discern God's voice and pray for people, I was not always certain it was God speaking to me. Three voices vie for our attention-our own, God's and Satan's. Therefore, we must learn to discern which voice is speaking. God's voice is always positive, affirming, corrective, encouraging and unrushed. God wants to direct, guide and teach us. Satan's voice, on the other hand, is negative, condemning and discouraging, and it may call for impulsive or hurried behavior. In order to discern God's voice, we must learn not only how to sort through our own thoughts but also the lies, temptations or other distractions that the enemy plants in our minds.

As you speak these words in a variety of prayer sessions, you become more adept at discerning if the words are your own, God's or Satan's. It is similar to being in a room full of people when someone walks in with whom you have an intimate relationship. You easily recognize the person's voice before you see him or her. When my wife Jane walks into a room, even though I may be in conversation with another, when she speaks I do not have to turn around to see who is speaking to me. I know it is she. In the same way, the more intimate your relationship is with the Lord, the easier it will be for you to recognize His voice.

GOD IS TRYING TO GET YOUR ATTENTION

Often, we can discern the voice of God without even realizing it. For example, I was receiving words of knowledge before I understood much about this gift. For nineteen years I was on staff of a large church in California. After the morning message the prayer teams would come to the front of the church, and people would come forward for prayer. Sometimes a word or picture would come into my mind that had absolutely nothing to do with what we were doing. I did not understand what was going on.

One Sunday morning in the midst of worship the word "kneecap" suddenly came into my mind. I was not thinking about my knee, it was not causing me any problems, and I was in the midst of trying to worship. While wondering what this was all about, I discerned the Lord prompting me to go up to the microphone and ask if anyone was having a problem with his or her knee. Nervously I walked up to the microphone and said what I believed the Lord was telling me. To my great surprise and relief, an individual came forward and said, "I believe that's me." As we gathered around him to pray, the Lord revealed further that the person had a hairline fracture in his kneecap. I shared this, and the person said, "I fell on this knee, and the doctor told me there was a hairline fracture but that little could be done." He was in pain and walking with a slight limp. As we prayed, the pain left and he walked back to his seat with no difficulty. Later as I shared this experience with someone much wiser and more experienced in spiritual gifts, he explained to me that I was receiving words of knowledge from the Lord.

There will be times when you may speak something you sense the Lord is giving you and no one will respond. Some are embarrassed or do not want to deal with what is being revealed. It is not unusual for people to find you later and say, "That was me you were receiving that word for. Can we still pray?" Rather than responding, "Nope, you lose buckwheat!" I always pray for people when they ask, knowing that it is not up to me to determine when the Lord should act or what He should do. We must be at the place where we are willing vessels ready to be used however and whenever God chooses.

AN EXERCISE IN LISTENING TO THE VOICE OF GOD

When I speak to groups on the subject of listening to God, I lead them in an exercise that helps them understand how to hear God's voice. I suggest that they break into small groups of three people who do not know each other. I ask that they not introduce themselves to each other or reveal any information about themselves to the group. I ask everyone to close his or her eyes, to be silent and completely still. No one should pray audibly at this point but should sit still before God in complete silence and wait for Him to speak. What He reveals may have to do with physical pain or sickness, a family problem, a relationship, emotional distress or a spiritual problem. No areas are off limits.

When they have gathered in their small groups of three and are ready to begin, I pray that God will reveal to each person in the room something specific that He wants him or her to pray for someone in the group. Without fail, eighty-five percent of the people report that God gave them a word or picture concerning someone in their group. When I ask them to share with each other what God said to them, the results are astounding! Almost without fail, someone in the group says, "That is exactly what I am dealing with and I have not shared that with you. There is no way you could have known that unless God revealed it to you!"

TWO AREAS OF DISCERNMENT

We need discernment in two major areas. The first is the discernment of God's truth. "Do your best to present yourselves to God as one approved, a workman who does not need to be ashamed and who correctly handles the word of truth" (2 Timothy 2:15). "All Scripture is God-breathed and is useful for teaching, rebuking, correcting and training in righteousness, so that the man of God may be thoroughly equipped for every good work" (2 Timothy 3:16-17).

It is imperative that we both listen to instruction in God's Word and spend time studying and dividing the Word of Truth for ourselves. The Spirit reveals to us how the Word applies in any given place or time. The same scripture may be used at different times in our lives with differing applications to our circumstances. Discernment is for this moment. We cannot apply given formulas from past experiences. If you have been a believer for any length of time and spent time in the Word of God, you know how often you can read the same passage over and suddenly it will come to life in a new way and fit the unique circumstance in which you find yourself.

The second area is that of God's direction, guidance and information for us personally. God communicates to us through thoughts, mental pictures, other people, nature, visions, dreams and an infinite variety of other ways. We must be wise in how we apply what we are hearing or seeing. Obviously, the message we hear must not contradict what God says in His Word. In most cases it will be instructive or edifying.

An important part of this type of discernment is in handling a word given to you by another. When someone comes to you with a prophetic word from the Lord, you must take it to God in prayer and ask that He confirm it. People are human and can make mistakes. Others can be using God's word to manipulate, and those who manipulate others for their own means can do serious damage to God's people. Therefore, it is wise to make sure that God is the One speaking. The confirmation may come very quickly, or it may take time. Wait for God so that you do not get ahead of Him.

Discernment Comes from Choosing to Listen

Discernment comes when we truly believe that God wants to communicate with us. John 10 equates this communication to that of the sheep and the shepherd. "His sheep follow Him because they know His voice. But they will never follow a stranger; in fact, they will run away from him because they do not recognize a stranger's voice" (verses 4,5). "My sheep listen to my voice; I know them, and they follow Me" (verse27). God not only talks in a voice we can hear, but He also expects us to learn to know His voice. Discernment comes with the choice to listen. We can shut these thoughts down if we choose. We usually make this choice when we do not choose to listen, when we do not know for certain it is God speaking, when we do not like what God is saying, or when we do not want to be obedient.

The Discerned Word Must Coincide with Scripture

As we mentioned briefly, God's Word should always be our reference book. It is our plumb line. He will never tell us anything contrary to His written word. When asking for guidance about a decision you need to make, you may read books and seek counsel from people who are hearing from God. But the final decision must line up with what you know to be God's truth. This will confirm that your discernment is sought from God and never from the enemy.

Slow Down, Tune Out the Static and Listen

"Be still and know that I am God" (Psalm 46:10). God does not speak to us until we slow down, tune out the static and give Him our attention. To walk in true discernment, our hearts must be quiet before God. We must learn how to wait and listen.

All true discernment comes through a heart that has ceased striving, a heart that knows, even in the fiery trial of its personal struggle, that the Lord is God. When you spend time with God and begin to take action based on what you believe you are hearing, you will see those actions confirmed either positively or negatively. Once you have said or done what He's telling you, once you risk taking action, the better you become at discerning whose voice you are hearing.

There is a jamming station that inhibits our powers of discernment. Our thoughts and reactions can block us from hearing God. We must die to personal judgments, ideas of retaliation and self-motivation. We must learn to listen to the voice of the Holy Spirit. As we stop our striving and listen, we discern. "He only is my rock, my salvation; I shall not be greatly shaken" (Psalms 62:2).

Listening is an art. Some of us are like Rembrandt-masters in the art-and some of us are like children in kindergarten-just beginning to finger-paint. But God will speak to us wherever we are in this learning process if we will simply stop and try to listen. He is not as interested in our ability as He is in our obedience.

5

THE TRAGEDY OF THE CHURCH TODAY

Everyone likes success. The messages of health, wealth, peace and prosperity emanate from our television screens, are spoken from our church pulpits and are communicated to us through Christian books and magazines. The underlying message is that Jesus intends for us to be "happy and prosperous," and if we are sick, worried, frustrated, anxious or not prosperous, something must be "wrong" with us.

In many churches, as in our culture, success is measured by growth. We look with admiration at the prosperous, vibrant, growing churches across America. If our church is not growing, we assume something is wrong. We are encouraged to follow the pattern of successful churches in our efforts to grow.

There is nothing inherently wrong with growth and prosperity. It is healthy and accomplishes much toward invading the kingdom of darkness with the kingdom of light. But we in the corporate Church have adopted unashamedly the techniques of the secular world to advertise, entice and exaggerate in order to lure people into the Church. The ethical climate easily becomes that of Wall Street, the moral climate that of Hollywood. We do not initiate as much as we imitate. Marketing madness drives us to read the latest book or attend the next seminar to learn what techniques we can use to accomplish more for the kingdom of God.

Somewhere in all of this striving for growth and prosperity, the simple message of the cross is buried. The love the Father has for us in our broken state is redefined. We believe our acceptance is based on what we do for Him, not who we are-His beloved. And losing this basic, fundamental message is a direct result of neglecting to spend time with our heavenly Father.

LOSING THE MESSAGE OF THE CROSS

If we were to closely examine the Church in America, would we see it as a significant force for change in our world? If we were honest with ourselves, the answer would likely be a resounding NO! Fortunately, it has not always been this way. There was a time when the Church was a force for change, both moral and ethical, but that voice has been muted significantly. In many countries it is costly and dangerous to be a Christian. In our country, however, it is not only easy, but little cost is involved. With our fast-paced programs and easy invitations to accept Jesus, the danger is that we have so watered down the cost that we have convinced people they can have all the benefits of the Gospel without any inconvenience to their way of life. In subtle ways the danger we face is how easily the message of the cross can become user-friendly.

The message requires no unpleasant lifestyle changes. The message makes no unpleasant demands. It does not slay the sinner but simply redirects him. When we examine the cross of historic Roman times, we discover that it stood for the abrupt, violent end of a human being. It did not try to keep on good terms with its victim. It never made concessions. It never compromised. When the cross finished its work, the victim was dead. "After Christ rose from the dead the apostles went out and preached the message of the cross. Wherever they went they preached the radical, revolutionary power of the cross. Christ crucified-Christ alive. That is the message that transformed Saul of Tarsus. That power remained as long as it was permitted to remain what it had been originally-a cross."[1]

In allowing the message of the cross to become so easily acceptable, we lose its true meaning. The message of the cross is not an improved old life but an entirely new life. In coming to Christ we do not bring our old life up onto a higher plane, we leave it at the cross-it is dead, you see. The message of the cross is not one of compromise. Rather, it is an ultimatum: "If anyone wishes to come after Me, let him deny himself, and take up his cross, and follow Me" (Matthew. 16:24). The cross destroys the first life and brings the old habits to an end. Then God raises the believer, and a new life begins.

"If you flee and ignore the cross you have nothing left but empty religious trappings because the power is gone. If we are to truly die upon it, we must be willing to submit the whole way we live our lives to be destroyed and built again in the power of an endless life. The cross will cut into our lives where it hurts, sparing neither us nor our carefully cultivated reputations."[2]

In contrast, when was the last time you heard this message in church? When was the last time you were taught that the cross of Christ is costly and involves suffering? Or when was the last time you were told that as Christians we must seek after, hunger for and thirst after the presence of God above all else?

FINDING SUITABLE TIME IN SOLITUDE WITH GOD

Perhaps we do not hear such messages because the words quietness, obedience, discipline, humility, simplicity and suffering are all foreign to our culture. They are not often spoken, and they are costly. Likewise, when someone speaks to us about silence and solitude, we respond, "I do not have time!" Thomas Kempis wrote, even before electricity or television had been invented, "If you avoid unnecessary talk and aimless visits, listening to news and gossip, you will find plenty of suitable time to spend in meditation on holy things."[3]

Many of us spend anywhere from six to twenty hours per week watching television. If we were to take the time we spend watching television and exchange it for solitude and quietness with God, do you think our lives would change? We spend time praying for God to send renewal or revival, and yet we are not willing to change our way of life. Rather than spend time with the very source of life, we create another program or find another task to accomplish that we trust will bring God's blessing.

We need this reformation as individuals, and we desperately need this reformation as the corporate Church. "To beg for a flood of blessing to come upon a backslidden and disobedient Church is a waste of time and effort. God is not interested in increased church attendance, unless those who attend amend their ways and begin to live holy lives."[4]

RELIGION AS AN OPIATE

It's been said that, "Without true, deep contemplative aspirations, without a total love of God and an uncompromising thirst for His truth, religion tends in the end to become an opiate."[5]

One of Webster's definitions for opiate is "Something that dulls the senses and induces relaxation."[6] Reflecting on what Thomas Merton said, it is not much of an intellectual stretch to see how religion can actually dull our spiritual senses and put us in a state where we are happy with the status quo. We can be in a place where we are not "hungering or thirsting" after God, where talk of contemplation, meditation or silence does not seem important. We have been lulled by our "religion" into a place of familiarity and complacency.

The idea of spending time with God just to listen and be

with Him did not appeal to me because I had not grasped the simple concept that if I want to build an intimate relationship with God I must spend time with Him. I was deluded in thinking that since I was doing all these great things for God we had a good, close relationship. Along the way there were times when I felt "caught up" into the presence of God and did not want to leave. But after returning from these mountaintop experiences, the daily grind of life would pull me back to reality. Once again, I would be caught up in the works mentality and settle back into my comfortable "religious place."

A person may be "religious" but at the same time be without the power of the cross, without the strength and conviction of one intimately acquainted with the Author of the message. Such a person might be locked into religion. Having attended church for years, he accepts Christian traditions as a part of life. Not much excites him, stirs him to delve deeper in his relationship with God, inflames him with passion for the mission field, or even compels him simply to pray.

"Religion as a dull habit is not that for which Christ lived and died."[7] But the tragedy is that for much of the Church, religion is a dull habit.

How easily our church attendance, our prayer lives and even our walks with God become no more than dull habits! Where is the man who has the "fire of God" in his belly, who is not content to simply go through the religious rituals, who is tired of playing church? Where are those asking, "Where is the Lord God of Elijah?" What could be more tragic than to miss understanding our belovedness, the wonder of holy obedience, and the delight of each day lived in the presence of God?

WHY DO WE SETTLE?

For many, life consists of one dreary day after another. People wake up in the morning, go to work, come home exhausted, watch a little television and then go to bed. They have no friends, no hobbies, no interests. They do not stop and smell the roses because they do not even notice the roses. The glass is never half-full-it is always half empty. God, if even acknowledged, is seen as uninvolved, unloving and uncaring. While the continuation of life may be acknowledged, it has little connection with God.

Why do we settle for life at a level that is so much less than what God intends for us? "Without doubt we have suffered the loss of many spiritual treasures because we have let slip the simple truth that the miracle of the perpetuation of life is in God. God did not create life and toss it from Him like some petulant artist disappointed with his work."[8]

Brennan Manning points out that perhaps we settle for life at a dreary level because of childhood memories that lay the pattern for self-deception. "These memories are so painful that we do not want to recall them or reveal them to anyone, so we keep them carefully concealed. When these voices from the past stir vague feelings of angry correction, which to us implies abandonment and rejection, we are certain that's what we are going to receive from God, so we avoid contact at all costs, or we sometimes settle for less because we are cowards." In writing about his own experience Manning said, "I have assumed a passive role in relationships, stifled creative thinking, denied my real feelings, allowed myself to be intimidated by others, and then rationalized my behavior by persuading myself that the Lord wants me to be an instrument of peace...at what price?"[9] In other words, we do not confront because we are fearful of being rejected or abandoned, so we do not allow our genuine selves to rise up to the place where God wants us to live, a place where God can transform us into the image of Jesus Christ.

In his book "Keys to the Deeper Life, A.W. Tozer says, "To speak of the deeper life is not to speak of anything deeper than simple New Testament religion. The deeper life is deeper only because the average Christian life is tragically shallow."[10] What an indictment! This was written in 1957. Imagine what Tozer would think if he were here to observe us today.

Why is our spiritual life so shallow? Part of the reason is that we are content in the shallows because it is safe, and we know that if we push beyond that place of contentment and go to the depths, there will be opposition and it will be costly. So, we are contented with a snack, and yet there is a complete feast awaiting us.

Additionally, we do not understand the privileges that are ours in Christ. We know intellectually that we are the King's Kids, but in reality we live as paupers. We are afraid to be exposed in the rags of our sinfulness, so we hide behind an impostor that keeps us locked in the prison of superficiality. We do not know by experience the precious, consuming presence of the Spirit of God.

FROM THE SHALLOWS TO THE DEPTHS

It is easy for us to say we want to be filled with the Spirit. Tragically, we have a limited understanding of what that means. A.W. Tozer asks, "Are you sure that you want to be possessed by a Spirit Who, while He is pure and gentle and wise and loving, will yet insist upon being Lord of your life? Are you sure you want your personality to be taken over by One Who will require obedience to the written Word? Who will not tolerate any of the self-sins in your life-self-love, self-indulgence? Who will not permit you to strut or boast or show off? Who will take the direction of your life away from you and will reserve the sovereign right to test you and discipline you? Who will strip away from you many loved objects which secretly harm your soul?"[11]

If we are to know the precious, consuming presence of the Spirit, we must spend time with Him. We must allow him to direct us, test and discipline us. To take those self-sins and bring us into complete obedience-obedience that causes us to acknowledge and surrender to Him as Lord over every part of our lives. This wholehearted surrender will take us from the shallows to the depths. It not only will transform our lives, but it also will radically change the face of the Church.

GOD CALLS US TO MUCH MORE THAN "NORMAL"

How deep and how rich are the ways of God! Is there any limit to what He can do? The obvious answer to this question is no. Emphatically NO! The more important question is, "Is there any limit to how much He can do with us, in us and through us?" The answer to this question is yes! We can limit God!

God will not violate our will. He is certainly able if He chooses, but He will not. He will not force us into relationship with Him. He will not force us into unfamiliar territory if we do not want to go. He will allow us to be status quo Christians if that is what we want.

Sadly, many Christians have no higher goal, no greater aspiration, than to be status quo. We like familiarity, we like routine, we like the "normal." We do not like to step out of the boat and walk on the water because it is scary and we might drown. Peter did not hesitate to step out of the boat, but once he realized where he was, he became afraid and wanted to get back in the boat because it was familiar. It was safe in the boat. There is nothing wrong with the familiar, but staying comfortable with those things that are normal and familiar keep us from experiencing the extraordinary. "If He would expand us to receive the eternal, He must rescue us from the limitations of the temporal."[12]

Jesus calls us to follow Him. Just as He called his disciples into unfamiliar territory, so we have been called to be alone with Him for extended periods of time. Francis Frangipane says, "We must understand: God does not want us "normal," He wants us Christlike!"[13]

To become Christlike, we must do the things that Christ did! His definition of normal would be far different from ours. He wants us to become familiar with Him, but God is so deep, so high, so wide, so entirely unfathomable to our finite minds that always we will be challenged to move further away from being comfortable, satisfied and normal. There is nothing normal about God.

OBEDIENCE AND HUMILITY

Meister Eckhart wrote: "There are plenty to follow our Lord half-way, but not the other half. They will give up possessions, friends and honors, but it touches them too closely to disown themselves."[14] When we begin to spend time with God, He reveals things about us that we do not want to give up-habits, interests, secret vanities, attitudes, prejudices-all those things about ourselves that we hide because if others knew about them they would be shocked, lose respect for us, or conclude that we are depraved, weak or of little value.

If we are going to move into an extraordinary place with God the Father we must allow Him to reveal to us all those hidden places and be willing to let Him change and purify us. This requires obedience and humility.

In John 13 Jesus gives us an example of humility by washing the feet of His disciples. In verse 14 He makes this astounding statement: "Now that I, your Lord and Teacher, have washed your feet, you also should wash one another's feet." Thomas Kempis addresses the importance of obedience and humility in his comments on John 13:14: "Is it so hard for you, who are dust and nothingness, to subject yourself to man for God's sake, when I, the Almighty and Most High, who created all things from nothing, humbly subjected Myself to man for your sake?"[15] We know Jesus had an extraordinary relationship with His Father and even though He was both "Lord and Teacher," He was willing to subject Himself to others in obedience and humility. Can we expect to do anything less?

Like Jesus, when we move into an intimate relationship with the Father, we will because of that relationship submit ourselves to man. Humility must be a part of us, as much a part of us as the air we breathe, and just as natural and unassuming. "Humility does not rest in final count upon bafflement and discouragement and self-disgust at our shabby lives, a brow-beaten, dog-slinking attitude. It rests upon the disclosure of the consummate wonder of God, upon finding that only God counts, that all our own self-originated intentions are works of straw."[16]

OBEDIENCE REQUIRES YIELDING

God willfully limits himself in His dealings with men. He set a boundary line in giving man free will. He sets the feast before us, but He will not compel us to eat. He opens the door into the abundant life, but He will not coerce us to enter. He places into the Bank of God a deposit that makes each of us a spiritual multimillionaire, but He will not write our checks. God has done His part, and we must do ours.

We must be willing to be obedient to Him-to yield to His will in our lives.

When we are driving down the road and see a Yield sign, normally we slow down and check out the traffic before we go bombing across the intersection. This is just common sense, right? If we are not willing to yield our rights at an intersection, it could cost us our lives.

Understanding this premise, then, why is it that in our daily lives we go casually along our way without yielding ourselves to what the Father wants to do with us or through us? We behave as if there are no consequences. We act as if we do not understand the necessity of yielding to Him, what is involved in yielding, or even how to yield. More importantly, we do not understand the consequences of not yielding.

Obedience is the road to intimacy, and intimacy comes through yielding. Before we can begin to experience intimacy with God, we must be willing to yield to Him. And we are not going to be willing to yield to Him if we do not trust Him or understand what yielding involves and what consequences we face if we do not yield.

It is up to us to make the decision to yield and be controlled by the Holy Spirit. God's twofold gift to us was not a partial gift. When He gave Christ, He gave all of Christ; and when He gave the Holy Spirit He gave all of the Holy Spirit. He withheld nothing from us. When God gave the Holy Spirit

He gave Him to indwell, infill and empower. He has provided us with the means whereby we are equipped to walk in confidence and power. But the responsibility to walk and live in the fullness of the Spirit is in our hands. You and I must make the decision whether we will yield or not.

He only gives as much as we allow Him to give. "As Savior He cannot save us from sin we insist upon retaining; as Head of the Body He cannot direct a stubborn member; as Lord He cannot reveal His will to one who does not want to know it or obey it; as Life He cannot fill what is already filled with a totally different substance; as Sanctifier He cannot separate us wholly unto Himself when we prefer to live unto self and the world; as Lord He cannot use us to defeat the enemy when we ourselves have already allowed him to defeat us." [17]

THE YIELDED LIFE

Paul tells us that once we choose to be obedient, Jesus Christ claims complete possession, control and use of our whole beings. "Do you not know that when you present yourselves to someone as slaves for obedience, you are slaves of the one whom you obey, either of sin resulting in death, or of obedience resulting in righteousness" (Romans 6:16). Knowing this, we should surrender to Him, not because we have to yield, but because we want to do so.

"Do you not know that your body is a temple of the Holy Spirit who is in you, whom you have from God and that you are not your own? For you have been bought with a price, therefore glorify God in your body" (1 Corinthians 6:19,20). At your conversion God laid claim to your body, and the Holy Spirit has already made it his home. He has a purpose in this. He wants to use you as a channel to reveal Himself to others, a channel to release His healing power, to reveal to men who He is and how much He loves them. (Romans 10:13-15)

Maybe you are sitting here thinking, "Okay, I'll do Him a favor and on occasion give Him the gift of some of my time or a part of my life for this moment." WRONG! You already belong to Him-he purchased claim to undivided possession and control. What right do we have to deny Him that which He purchased?

Or, perhaps you have been thinking, "Must I do this?" But the question ought to be, "Will I yield to Him who gave His all for me?" You see, we do not yield in order to be His but, rather, because we are His. Our purchase by His blood gives Him title, delivery and possession. "Have you yielded to God what already belongs to Him? Can we not trust the One who died for us? "He who did not spare His own Son, but delivered Him up for us all, how will He not also with Him freely give us all things?" (Romans 8:32).

We may have some idea what a life yielded to God will be like, but I think it is important to first observe what it is not. It is not merely holding to a particular belief. It is not merely the saving of our souls. It is not simply giving oneself to a particular kind or field of service. It is not just stopping evil practices, nor praying and reading your Bible. It is giving Him our whole selves-our bodies, our members, our being. It includes everything-mind, emotions, will, home, families, possessions, occupation, friendship, time, money, goals, the past, present, future, our worst and our best. It is the glad, joyous, willing response of love to love.

Like all things of great value, there is a cost. I read this quote in a church bulletin:

OTHERS MAY, YOU CANNOT

"If God has called you to be really like Jesus in all your spirit, He will draw you into a life of crucifixion and humility and put on you such demands of obedience that He will not allow you to follow other Christians, and in many ways He will seem to let other good people do things that He will not let you do.

Other Christians and ministers who seem very religious and useful may push themselves, pull wires and work schemes to carry out their plans, but you cannot do it; and if you attempt it, you will meet with such failure and rebuke from the Lord as to make you sorely penitent.

Others can brag on themselves, on their work, on their success, on their writings, but the Holy Spirit will not allow you to do any such thing, and if you begin it, He will lead you into some deep mortification that will make you despise yourself and all your good works.

Others will be allowed to succeed in making money, or having a legacy left to them or in having luxuries, but it is likely God will keep you poor, because He wants you to have something far better than gold, and that is a helpless dependence upon Him, that He may have the privilege of supplying your needs day by day out of an unseen treasury.

The Lord will let others be honored and put forward, and keep you hid away in obscurity, because He wants to produce some choice, fragrant fruit for His coming glory, which can only be produced in the shade.

God will let others be great, but keep you small. He will let others do a work for Him and get the credit for it, but He will make you work and toil on without knowing how much you are doing; and then to make your work still more precious, He will let others get the credit for the work you have done, and this will make your reward ten times greater when Jesus comes. The Holy Spirit will put a strict watch over you, with a jealous love, and will rebuke you for little words and feelings or for wasting your time, which other Christians never seem distressed over.

So make up your mind that God is an infinite Sovereign and has a right to do as He pleases with His own, and He will not explain to you a thousand things that may puzzle your reason in His dealings with you. God will take you at your word; and if you absolutely sell yourself to be His slave, He will wrap you up in a jealous love and let other people say and do many things that you cannot do or say.

Settle it forever, that you are to deal directly with the Holy Spirit, and that He is to have the privilege of tying your tongue or chaining your hand, or closing your eyes in ways that others are not dealt with. Now when you are so possessed with the living God that you are in your secret heart pleased and delighted over this peculiar, personal, private, jealous guardianship and management of the Holy Spirit over your life, you will have found the vestibule of heaven."[18]

REFUSING TO YIELD

Refusal to yield any part is an act of rebellion. There is a direct correlation between the extent to which God will use us and our willingness to yield ourselves to Him to be used.

We cannot just bring the troublesome, unmanageable parts of our lives to God, asking Him for spiritual repairs while we do what we want. We are like the man I read about who took the hands of his clock to the jeweler and asked him to regulate them, as they did not keep time. "Bring me the whole clock," said the jeweler, "the cause of the inaccuracy is not in the hands." "No!" said the owner, "you will take it all to pieces and it will cost me a lot! It is the hands that go wrong!"

Maybe we find it difficult to believe that God can accept us because there is so much bad in our lives. Or perhaps we have no difficulty in bringing to God the sins but see no reason to yield the best-"Why do I need to ask the Lord, if I can use my own good sense? I know as well as He how to do it." Or we reserve some areas for ourselves-we offer substitutes. We bribe him with our time, talents or service in lieu of yielding ourselves.

Are you just bringing God the hands? The refusal to yield any part, however insignificant it may seem, is an act of rebellion and will make it difficult to experience the fullness of the Holy Spirit in our lives.

If you think this is an impossible journey, be assured it is not. Accept and recognize the wounds, the shame and the fear. In some sense or another, we all project a false self in order to be accepted by God and others. Brennan Manning says, "The tendency to construct a self-image based on performing religious acts leads to the illusion of self-righteousness...we lose touch with the true self and the happy combination of mysterious dignity and pompous dust which we really are."[19]

God does not wait for perfection. Wherever you are in your spiritual walk, if you can begin to submit yourself to Him and spend time with Him, then God will use your whole journey. Do not be discouraged by the small amount of time you may give in the beginning. If you slip and stumble, do not spend much time in regret and blame, do not let the enemy deceive you by saying, "You cannot do this, you are not worthy, or you do not have enough time for this." Thomas Kelly so eloquently says, "Don't grit your teeth and clench your fists and say, "I will! I will!" Relax. Take hands off. Submit yourself to God. Learn to live in the passive voice and let life be willed through you. For "I will" spells not obedience."[20]

Maintain the Message

If the message of the cross is to be understood in such a way as to bring death to our old way of life, then there is no gentle, palatable way for the message to be presented. But although it is not gentle, this same message brings us into life and power.

If we, the Corporate Church, are to become a significant force for change in our world we must declare this message. We must not use religion as an opiate. Rather, we must have an uncompromising thirst for the Truth, we must never allow ourselves to be comfortable and "normal," and we must be willing to yield ourselves entirely to God. And it is only through individual Christians doing these things that the Corporate Church will be changed.

6

THE FOOLISHNESS OF GOD

Paul tells us that the Gospel message we have is foolishness and that we are to preach the power of this message: "For the message of the cross is foolishness to those who are perishing, but to us who are being saved it is the Power of God" (1 Corinthians 1:18). So not only must we spend time with Him, but we must proclaim and demonstrate the message. While it is a message of Good News, change and hope, it is a message that does not make sense to our world: To live we must die; to receive we must give; to be exalted we must humble ourselves.

Proclaiming and demonstrating this message is what we are called to do as children of God. If we are to demonstrate that this is a message of power, not only must we speak in the power and authority we have been given (Matthew 28:18,19), but we also must demonstrate what John Wimber referred to as "power evangelism." In Acts 8:5-8 we read the story of Philip going down to Samaria to proclaim Christ. In verses 6 and 7 we read, "When the crowds heard Philip and saw the miraculous signs he did, they all paid close attention to what he said. With shrieks, evil spirits came out of many, and many paralytics and cripples were healed." If we are to evangelize in such a powerful way as Philip did, we must spend time with God building intimacy through relationship. There is no shortcut to the power of God.

Today, in the eyes of many, the Church is an object of ridicule-not only because the message seems so foolish, but also because they see little demonstration of the power of God in the lives of many Christians. Some say we have a foolish God and a foolish message. Many think we Christians are weak and foolish. Those who do not believe there is a God at all think we are extremely foolish to live our lives by the teaching of One whom they believe does not exist. "The message that points to Christ on the cross seems like sheer silliness to those hell-bent on destruction, but for those on the way of salvation it makes perfect sense. This is the way God works, and most powerfully as it turns out" (1 Corinthians 1:18, *The Message*).

The basic message of the cross seems to our world to be out of touch with reality and of little use to us in our daily lives. In our sophisticated world of advertising and marketing strategy, even the method by which this message was originally delivered and communicated makes little sense. A legitimate question might be: "If this message was so important, with eternal consequence for each of us, why would God use His Son Jesus and a ragtag group of simple men to communicate this message to the world?"

GOD'S MESSAGE AND PLAN

God had a two-part plan regarding this message. First, God had a design for redeeming mankind from the sentence of death and bringing us back into intimate relationship with Himself (John 3:16). His plan was to take His Son and send Him into the world among the nobodies to tell them the Good News, a message that would change the world. He allowed his Son to be nailed to a cross, the symbol of complete helplessness and death, and then He raised Jesus from the dead and took Him back to heaven to be with Him.

Then came the second part of the plan. While Jesus was on earth, He was to disciple a band of men who, for the most part, were uneducated and of little standing in the eyes of the world. Then after His death and resurrection He was to leave them behind, instructing them to take the simple message of the cross to the whole world: "Christ was crucified for your sins." By proclamation and demonstration Jesus' disciples were to share this message, which we are told is a gift to us from God. We do not have to earn it or prove ourselves worthy in any way. We cannot write a check for it. We simply accept that our redemption from death was given totally by the grace and mercy of God. He forgives our sin, fills us with His Spirit and gives us this gift of eternal life because He loves us. We cannot earn this love by anything we do or do not do. Quite simply, we are His beloved. That is our core identity.

Sounds too good to be true, right? Would the marketing strategists of the world do it this way? A marketing proposal like this would be laughed out of the corporate boardroom. "Can this sell?" Is it "seeker friendly?" To the world this is foolishness! But this was God's plan and the strategy He decided to use.

If we had a message we wanted to communicate to the entire world, one we knew could impact millions of people, how would we plan it? Imagine a corporate boardroom with influential men and women around a table developing the most effective strategy for communicating this life-changing message. The first step of the plan probably would require obtaining large amounts of money for this worthy cause. They then would look for the brightest and sharpest people within their own organizations to implement the plan.

In addition, they would contact those within their spheres of influence who have name recognition, power and authority to make things happen. Jerry Lewis is a good example of this principle at work. When you hear his name, what do you think of? Typically he is associated with the Muscular Dystrophy telethon. We all have seen Jerry standing by children in wheelchairs, encouraging us to give our support.

"This is a disease we can lick together, we need you to give now." This worthy organization is doing it right. It is getting results and accomplishing its goals with high quality people, programming and advertising.

Organizations operating like this one make everybody look and feel like a winner. The stars are winners because they are giving freely of their time, you are a winner for supporting the organization, and the children are going to be winners because of your help. This is the way things are accomplished in the world.

But the Scriptural message we have received and the way in which we are to proclaim it is quite different from this worldly scenario. The world through its wisdom did not know Him. They were looking for miraculous signs and wonders, or wisdom in all the wrong places. "So where can you find someone truly wise, truly educated, truly intelligent in this day and age? Hasn't God exposed it all as pretentious nonsense? Since the world in all its fancy wisdom never had a clue when it came to knowing God, God in his wisdom took delight in using what the world considered dumb-preaching, of all things!-to bring those who trust Him into the way of salvation. While Jews clamor for miraculous demonstrations and Greeks go for philosophical wisdom, we go right on proclaiming Christ the Crucified. Jews treat this like an anti-miracle, and Greeks pass it off as absurd. But to us who are personally called by God himself-both Jews and Greeks-Christ is God's ultimate miracle and wisdom all wrapped up in one" (1 Corinthians 1:20-24, *The Message*).

Jesus had His disciples preach a message of Christ Crucified and demonstrate the power of the message. "You want to live, you have to die; you want to receive, you have to give up. Human wisdom is so tiny, so impotent, next to the seeming absurdity of God. Human strength cannot begin to compete with God's weakness" (1 Corinthians 1:25, *The Message*).

What the world sees as foolishness we read in Scripture is "wiser than all of man's wisdom!" All the wisdom and plans of man; the multitude of ways the world believes we can attain health, wealth, peace and prosperity; when we are told that through meditation we can transcend this material universe and channel into the essence of what is, even becoming our own God-we Christians should be able to see that these worldly messages are foolishness when compared with the message of the cross. God's message is indeed a message of life, a message demonstrated through lives that are radically healed and changed.

PEACE, MY BROTHER

I remember well the decade of the '60s. I was living in San Francisco during the height of this movement and was quite enchanted with the entire peace and love scene. I did not dress like the typical longhaired flower child with tie-dyed T-shirts and bell-bottomed pants, but I certainly liked what they were doing and participated in the movement. I recall many days walking around Haight-Ashbury and Golden Gate Park, where the smells of incense and sounds of sitar music drifted through the air-a place where moon-eyed, long-haired girls would hand you a flower as they smilingly said, "Peace, my brother." You could walk into the park near the end of Haight Street, sit down on the grass with a group of people you did not know and share their food, wine and talk of peace as they passed the pipe around. It was a fairy-tale time. It was a time in my life when I was examining everything-my religious beliefs, values, political beliefs-everything. I remember thinking at one point, *Perhaps this can work and we can all get along. Perhaps this will bring me the self-contentment I desperately need. Perhaps inner peace is possible.*

But then, just as suddenly as it began, this scene started to turn ugly. As I began to get below the surface of love and peace, I saw greed, envy and jealousy. I saw the ugliness and destruction of lives brought about by free love and drugs. I saw kids with minds blown away by LSD, begging in the streets for food, willing to sell their bodies for a warm place to sleep. Most importantly, I saw that this definitely was not the way to find peace with myself, God or anyone else. At the age of 24, I was at the lowest point I had ever been both emotionally and spiritually. Living on a sailboat I remember thinking, *I'll just sail off into the sunset and check out of this whole scene. Surely there is something better elsewhere.*

I was twelve when I became a Christian and now twelve years later, I was facing something I could not handle. God had me right where He wanted me. At this low point in my life I came back home. I met with a friend of mine who was a strong Christian. I did not know where else to go. As we prayed together, I vividly remember saying, "Lord I do not understand what's going on, I do not even know if you are really there, but if you are, I need you to show me, and I give myself to you, as much as I know how, to do with as you want."

I immediately felt this warm wind and was overwhelmed with such a feeling of warmth and peace that words are not adequate to describe it. I looked up at my friend who was praying with me and said, "Did you feel that?" He said, "Yes." I knew without a doubt that God loved me personally, listened to me and cared about what I was going through. This was a defining moment in my life. It was the first step in the journey of learning how to live in God's peace. Certainly there have been times since then when I have been afraid. Sometimes I have not been sure what was going on, what God was doing or what was going to happen to me. But rarely since then have I doubted God would do and be exactly what He said He would do and be.

GOD'S MESSAGE VS. THE WORLD'S MESSAGE

In San Francisco among the flower children, there were numerous ways to peace and tranquility. There was marijuana and hashish to make us mellow yellow. There was Timothy Leary and his LSD to expand our minds and help us get in touch with the depths of our souls, moving into deeper oneness with our unconsciousness. Many did this quite successfully and are still in that state of mind. There was the Maharishi Mahesh Yogi who wanted to help us get in touch with our inner selves and commune with the oneness of who we are-whatever that means! But this "wisdom of man" did not end with the close of the flower child generation. The message simply has metamorphosed into other forms.

Today health, wealth, peace and prosperity rain down upon us from various media sources. Some televangelists assure us that when we plant the right seed in the right place, we will reap a bountiful harvest of health and wealth. The marketing experts tell us that if we wear the right clothes, use the right deodorant and eat the right food, life will be more fun and people will like us. Some of the messages of the '60s hang around in the form of New Age pluralism, and many of our popular movie personalities espouse a form of this pluralism in promoting their religion, which usually has nothing to do with the God of Scripture. Based on what we see or hear from role models, heroes, leaders or other significant people in our lives, we have come to believe that it is okay to use some recreational drugs; it is okay to engage in illicit sex as long as you do it safely; it is okay to be gay because "God made you that way;" it is okay to have abortions because women have a right to make any choice concerning their bodies; and on and on.

Consider the world's messages against the message of the cross. Which of them sounds the most foolish? To human ears, the truths of the Gospel sound like foolishness because of their very simplicity. They are equally free to the unlearned as to the highly educated. They set aside self-righteous works. The Gospel message offends religious pride because a cross is such a sign of helpless weakness that it seems impossible for it to be the mechanism of divine, saving power.

And whom does God use? Not those who by the standards of the world are wise, influential or of high society. He bypasses those who trust in themselves and their own strength and wisdom. Rather, God uses the weak, the lowly, the nobodies to shame the wise and the strong. "Brothers, think of what you were when you were called. Not many of you were wise by human standards, not many were influential; not many were of noble birth. But God chose the foolish things of the world to shame the wise; God chose the weak things of the world to shame the strong. He chose the lowly things of this world and the despised things and the things that are not to nullify the things that are, so that no one may boast before Him" (1 Corinthians 1: 26-29).

This same passage in *The Message* reads, "Take a good look, friends, at who you were when you got called into this life. I do not see many of the 'brightest and the best' among you, not many influential, not many from high-society families. Isn't it obvious that God deliberately chose men and women whom the culture overlooks and exploits and abuses, chose these 'nobodies'? That makes it quite clear that none of you can get by with blowing your own horn before God" (1 Corinthians 1:26-29, *The Message*). The message itself is foolishness to the world, and its advocates-those of us viewed not as movers and shakers, not as influential or of high society but, rather, as the weak and lowly-are considered fools.

THE ARMY

Scripture teaches that we are participating in a battle with evil (Ephesians 6:12), that we are warriors in an army (Ephesians 6:10-11) and that He gave us the Spirit of the Lord (2 Timothy 1:7; Isaiah 11:2), who is wisdom, understanding, counsel, knowledge, power and peace. First Corinthians 1:26-31 provides a description of this army. This passage describes five categories: the foolish, the weak, the lowly, the despised and the nobodies. This is the way the world views us. In this army the fools are in the front line, and the weak are in the second line.

Perhaps you have been thinking you were too unqualified for proclaiming and demonstrating the message of the cross? WRONG! You are perfect for this army. Step up right behind the fools, who are such fools that they are not ashamed to be in the front line! If you are weak, get in the second row. And if you are not good enough for the second row, then step right up behind the lowly, the despised and the nobodies.

Is this the group that is ordered to take charge and break the enemy line? Is the message of the cross their only weapon? Yes. And we are strong-stronger and more invincible than any worldly way, for hidden within our contemptible exterior is the all-victorious presence of Christ and the irresistible power of the Holy Spirit.

We may not look like much on the outside, but we are children of the Most High God! Galatians says we are "chosen, adopted, sealed and given a deposit guaranteeing our inheritance" (1:4). In Ephesians we are described as "His workmanship created in Christ Jesus to do good works" (2:10). In 1 Corinthians we are a temple and we belong to God, for "He paid for us with His Son's blood" (3:16, 19-20). In Romans we are "heirs of God and co-heirs with Christ" (8:17). Romans also tells us, "If God is for us, who can be against us?" (8:31).

If this were not enough, Scripture tells us we also have the Holy Spirit and His gifts. When you receive Jesus Christ you receive the Holy Spirit. You determine by obedience or disobedience how God will work through you and manifest His gifts. He will choose their time and place to manifest, but you decide whether or not you will allow Him to use you to manifest these gifts of the Holy Spirit.

If Scripture is to be believed, then we have spiritual gifts, the armor of God, Jesus interceding for us, and the Holy Spirit interceding for us. We are God's empowered, chosen, set apart people!

And yes, this message is our only weapon. But this is not a message of small consequence. This is a message about changed lives, healed bodies, restored families, a revolutionized nation and world. We have the privilege of proclaiming and demonstrating the message of the foolishness of God to the world!

PROCLAIMING THE MESSAGE

But how does this army best proclaim and demonstrate this foolish message? How do we persuade others that it is indeed a message of power, transformation and healing that will change lives dramatically?

Most of the Church does not have a problem proclaiming the Word. In fact, the Word of God is often "preached." The American Heritage dictionary defines *preach*: "to exhort in an officious or tiresome manner."[1] *Officious* means "to volunteer one's services where they are neither asked for nor needed."[2] The message of the cross is spoken in many places, but often it is rendered in a tiresome manner where it is not asked for, nor wanted.

We are called to do more than preach the Gospel. What we are called to do under the power of the Holy Spirit is to proclaim this message and to demonstrate it by our lives. That is not tiresome! In fact, when people see that we are doing what we are saying, they will come. When people see someone healed they are seeing the presence of the authority of God (Mark 16:17). When they see someone saved, or when they see the Spirit of God poured out, they are seeing the Kingdom of God breaking into the kingdom of darkness (Colossians 1:13). These signs are proofs of the Kingdom of God.

When we tell people about the message of the cross and do not demonstrate the power of that message by praying for the sick, when we stifle the moving of the Holy Spirit through fear or ignorance, or when we do not teach the people of God how to do what Jesus did, we are walking in disobedience! If the Gospel is indeed Good News, then power must accompany the message! In Matthew 10:7-8 Jesus said, "The Kingdom of heaven is near. Heal the sick, raise the dead, cleanse those who have leprosy, drive out demons." This world needs to see demonstrations of God's Power. How else are we going to get people's attention? How are we going to pull our young people away from the grip the Devil has on them through drugs, sex and music. How else are we going to fight the New Age movement, the gay rights movement, the abortion movement, the Humanist movement?

People have not changed in 2,000 years. They are still

asking the same questions and looking for something real in their lives. People need signs and wonders. They need to hear testimonies from those who have been released from the grip of the devil. People who are in this dead place, who are ignorantly headed toward hell and do not even know it, need to be able to come to a point where they ask, "What is this you are saying and doing? Is this what God is like? Is this message the answer I am looking for? If this is real, tell me about Jesus!"

The proclamation and demonstration of the message of the cross is what the world sees as the foolishness of God! Proclaiming this message and, more importantly, demonstrating it in our lives is what we are called to do as children of God.

But before any of this can happen we need to do three things that in the eyes of the world are foolish. First, place Jesus back on the throne of our lives. He must be the focus, the central point in our lives. Our entire reason for living must be to please Him. Nothing else can be on the throne-not our goals, our needs, our agenda or even our ministry-only Jesus.

Second, we must spend time with God building intimacy through worship, Scripture, solitude and silence. He must become our dearest friend whom we trust completely and with whom we can be totally transparent. There is no shortcut to building this depth of relationship. The only way to have a deep, intimate relationship with the Lord is to spend significant time with Him.

Third, understand to what we have been called. That is, to preach the Gospel, cast out demons, heal the sick, release the oppressed and be Jesus to the world. Do what Jesus did and do it with boldness!

7

WHEN IT IS OKAY TO BE A CHILD

Childlikeness is the pathway to intimacy. When my granddaughter comes to my house she wants to play with Grandma or Grandpa. This can go on for hours. If she has to play by herself she will, but it is much more fun to play with one of us. Just to be with us, to hang out and have some fun is the reason she likes to come over to our house. I believe that part of the reason why we do not hang out with God is that we feel our time is too valuable to be used in this way. We have grown up and decided that the most valuable use of our time with God is to be doing something for Him. Truthfully, many of us feel this is why God loves us. Sadly, we have lost the childlike innocence of openness and transparency with our Father God.

Throughout Scripture believers are referred to as children. For example, Matthew 5, one of the most familiar passages in the Bible, says, "Blessed are the peacemakers for they shall be called the children of God" (verse 9). John writes, "Now dear children, continue in Him so that when He appears we may be confident and unashamed before Him at His coming" (1 John 2:28).

For us the concept of little children conjures images of noise, constant movement, fussing, unbridled enthusiasm, self-centeredness, selfishness, openness, honesty and total trust. But we see children from a different perspective than Jesus did. Childlikeness and childishness are two very different things. Jesus' perspective is best seen in a conversation He had with His disciples, who ask Him, "Who then is greatest in the kingdom of heaven?" (Matthew 18:1). It seems obvious they had been talking about their rank and status in the coming kingdom. In a companion passage in Mark, He directly asks them, "What were you arguing about on the road, but they kept quiet because on the way there they had argued about who was the greatest" (Mark 9:33-34). Jesus took a little child and had him stand among them and said, "I tell you the truth, unless you change and become like little children, you will never enter the kingdom of heaven...Therefore whoever humbles himself like this child is the greatest in the kingdom of heaven" (Matthew.18:3,4). A little child has no idea that he is great. In the kingdom of heaven, the greatest is he who is least conscious of being great. Our trust, openness and eagerness regarding the things of God exhibit this childlike behavior.

Therese of Lisieux said, "It is recognizing one's nothingness, expecting everything from the good God, just as a little child expects everything from its father; it is not getting anxious about anything, not trying to make one's fortune...Being little is also not attributing to oneself the virtues that one practices, as if one believed oneself capable of achieving something, but recognizing that the good God puts this treasure into the hands of His little child for it to make use of it whenever it needs to; but it is always the good God's treasure. Finally it is never being disheartened by one's faults, because children often fall, but they are too little to do themselves much harm."[1]

THE HONESTY OF CHILDREN

Children are capable of realizing they need help. When things become overpowering they have no problem calling out for help. Children realize they have limitations, but those limitations actually cause them to seek help in solving the problem or in reaching the next level they want to achieve.

One of the dangers of "growing up" is that we can lose this childlikeness and become adults who are critical, distrustful, hypocritical, unloving or rigid. In Luke Jesus tells the parable of the children at play in the marketplace. "To what then shall I compare the men of this generation, and what are they like?" They are like children who sit in the marketplace and call to one another; and they say, "We played the flute for you, and you did not dance; we sang a dirge, and you did not weep" (Luke 7:31,32). These children did not know what they wanted, except they all wanted their own way. "In this case Jesus depicts the most unattractive characteristic of immaturity-the trifling, fickle, uncooperativeness of a bored, spoiled child. The children in the marketplace were really saying, 'If you do not do what I want, I won't do what you want. But I do not even know what I want. If you were to do what I think I want, I am not sure even that would please me!'"[2]

Jesus is saying that this generation is like that bored, spoiled child. Of course, children are not outstanding examples of humility, and they certainly can be just like those described above. But children also can be incredibly honest and trusting. Jesus is pointing out that we can possess the humility necessary for entrance into the kingdom of heaven if we are prepared to come as little children who are open, trusting and unashamed. Jesus said, "It is easier for a camel to go through the eye of a needle than for a *rich* man to enter the kingdom of God" (Matthew 19:24, NLT, emphasis mine). We could just as easily insert the words *proud, distrustful, apathetic* and *fearful* to describe many of us. He points out that if you are prepared to be as open, enthusiastic, honest and trusting as little children, you can enter the kingdom of heaven. "The life that intends to be wholly obedient, wholly submissive, wholly listening, is astonishing in its completeness. Its joys are ravishing, its peace profound, its humility the deepest, its power world-shaking, its love enveloping, its simplicity that of a trusting child."[3]

THE SENSITIVITY AND OPENNESS OF CHILDREN

In Matthew people were trying to bring the little children to Jesus, and the disciples were trying to prevent them from gaining access to Him. Jesus uses this as an opportunity to teach a vital truth about the character of the members of the kingdom of God: "Then some children were brought to Him so that He might lay His hands on them and pray; and the disciples rebuked them. But Jesus said, 'Let the children alone, and do not hinder them from coming to Me; for the kingdom of heaven belongs to such as these.' And after laying His hands on them He departed from there" (Matthew. 19:13-15).

The children heard the same words as the adults, but they heard, believed and accepted. They were open to receive the truth, not analyze the trust. They were open to accept the word for themselves.

Jesus was fully aware of the children's frailties. Nevertheless, He undoubtedly knew that, though far from innocent, they were more sensitive to the supernatural world than adults tend to be. It is easier for children to see God's hand directly at work in His creation. Often what adults regard as ordinary things are considered by children to be matters of great significance.

One of the delights of being a "grandpa" is when my granddaughter goes with me into our yard to cut roses. She gleefully runs from bush to bush yelling, "Look at the pretty roses God made for us!" Sadly, we often go through life not stopping to notice the roses. Our childlike enthusiasm may have been dulled to such a degree that we no longer enjoy the wonder of God's creation. We may have vision, but no sight to see the simple things of life that God uses to speak and share with us.

RETAINING CHILDLIKE QUALITIES

In these passages from Matthew, Jesus is not encouraging His disciples to be childish. What He is saying is that we do not have to lose these childlike qualities when we grow up. It has been said, "The kingdom of God, He implies, belongs to those who are trustful, receptive and friendly, and who remain unspoiled by the difficulties and disillusionments, the cynicism and the pessimism, the compromises and the deceptions that so often depress and disfigure adult life."[4] He wants us to retain those childlike qualities that make us receptive to what the Father says and does.

Think about the wonder, receptiveness and un-sophistication of children. "A child is dependent and trusting-at least until adult unworthiness breaks the trust. A child is friendly and unconscious of status or race-until adult prejudice spoils that relationship. A child is candid, as witnessed in the Hans Christian Andersen story of the emperor's new clothes-the adults admired them, not daring to say anything different until a little child said, 'But he has nothing on!' A child lives in constant wonder, makes toys out of trash and finds life a high romance. A child expects great things of life and finds them."[5]

The faith that Jesus prized is instinct in a child. As William McNamera would say, "The lost quality of childlikeness can be enjoyed only by unspoiled children, *uncanonized saints*, undistinguished sages and unemployed clowns" (emphasis mine).[6]

BEING CHILDLIKE: A DOORWAY INTO RELATIONSHIP

Why is it so important to be as a child? Children are open, trusting, authentic, honest, uninhibited in their expressions and spontaneous in their emotions. Brennan Manning writes, " The positive qualities of a child-openness, trusting dependence, playfulness, simplicity, sensitivity to feelings-restrain us from closing ourselves off to new ideas, unprofitable commitments, the surprises of the Spirit and risky opportunities for growth. The unself-consciousness of the child keeps us from morbid introspection, endless self-analysis and the fatal narcissism of spiritual perfectionism."[7]

When we rediscover that we are "the beloved," we can "preserve childlike innocence through unflagging awareness of the core identity and by steadfast refusal to be intimidated and contaminated by peers."[8] Such peers are often those people in our lives who prevent us from being real. They may intimidate us with their athletic prowess, intellectual achievements and artistic talents. These are the peers "whose lives are spent not in living but in courting applause and admiration; not blissfully being themselves but in neurotically comparing and competing, striving for those empty things called success and fame even if they can be attained only at the expense of defeating, humiliating or destroying their neighbors."[9]

Until we break out of the mold created by the expectations of others, we will not become childlike in our wonder of God's creation, nor will we sense an awe of God our Creator. And we will not grasp what God has done for us personally. A. W. Tozer had a childlike perspective as he eloquently grasped the magnitude of this personal redemption: "For me prophet wrote and psalmist sang. For me holy men spake as they were moved by the Holy Ghost. For me Christ died, and the redemptive benefits of that death are by the miracle of His present life perpetuated forever, as efficacious now as on the day He bowed His head and gave up the ghost. And when He arose the third day it was for me; and when He poured out upon the disciples the promised Holy Spirit it was that He might continue in me the work He had been doing for me since the morning of the creation."[10]

Becoming like a child is not simply an end in itself. Rather, it is more like a doorway to our union with God. Being childlike means going deep emotionally, being sensitive, being spiritually connected and knowing that we are His beloved and are held by Him. Frederick Buechner writes, "We are children, perhaps, at the very moment when we know that it is as children that God loves us-not because we have deserved His love and not in spite of our undeserving; not because we try and not because we recognize the futility of our trying; but simply because He has chosen to love us."[11]

Things that Keep Us from Childlikeness

Not Understanding the Father's Love

A part of what keeps us from this childlikeness is failing to understand the Father's love for us. The Father God loves you as much as He loves His Son Jesus! Such a concept is hard for us to comprehend since we see ourselves as weak sinners who are full of evil, ugly things.

When ministering at a maximum-security prison, I gave an invitation for the men to open their hearts to receive Jesus' forgiveness of their sins and accept Him as Lord of their lives. Some of them responded, and later as I was talking to one of the prisoners I noticed another prisoner tentatively making his way up the aisle toward me. As he neared where I was standing he reached out and tugged at my shirtsleeve. I turned around and he said, "Can I ask you a question?" I replied, "Of course." He asked, "When Jesus forgave me of my sins did He forgive me of all of them?" I said, "Yes." "You mean all of them?" "Yes." Slowly shaking his head in disbelief as he turned to walk away, I heard him say, "Wow, all of them!" It was so hard for this man to comprehend that Jesus had forgiven him of all of his sins. For him, this was an experience of the Father's agape love-unconditional acceptance and forgiveness.

> *"But God demonstrates his own love for us in this; while we were still sinners, Christ died for us" (Romans 5:8).*

Holding Back our Emotions

Agape love is a foundational truth among Christians. But another part of the Father's love is also often difficult for adults to receive: *phileo,* which means "demonstrated tender affection for us." Isaiah says, "He tends His flock like a shepherd; He gathers the lambs in His arms and carries them close to His heart; He gently leads those that have young" (Isaiah 40:11). The focus is more on a touch from God, on feelings. Most women seem to more easily be able to get in touch with and express their feelings, but men often have a more difficult time expressing feelings. Men may think it is unmanly to show feelings or feel warm fuzzies. Sometimes our feelings are shut down because of things that have happened to us. Regrettably this means we also find it difficult to feel the love of our Father God.

These walls keep us from knowing God intimately. As adults we tend to see God at a distance. Children have no problem running up to someone and saying, "I want to sit on your lap." They may stop what they are doing, run over and tell you they need a hug. Such an action is quite difficult for adults because we tend to hold back our emotions for fear of rejection.

Those emotions were created as a part of our basic makeup, but unfortunately this emotional touch of love is missing from the lives of many Christians. We need His affectionate touch, affirming words and the blessing of the Father, for these are healing to our souls.

Not Having the Heart of a Child

Central to receiving affection is a heart turned toward God in childlike trust. "Man looks on the outward appearance, but the Lord looks at the heart" (1 Samuel 16:7). The heart is not only the center of our physical life, but it is also the center of the spiritual nature of man. It is the center of powerful emotions, enthusiasm and sexual desire. When we do something gladly, willingly and with determination it is done from the heart. It is common for us to express appreciation for musicians or athletes when we say, "He played his heart out!" The heart is also described as the seat of love and hatred, of feelings and affections that can range from joy to absolute terror.

What does God see when He looks at your heart? What passion do you have for God? Do you delight in spending time with Him, in weeping with Him, in laughing with Him? Many of us are like a frightened little boy afraid of being found out, rather than a child delighted to run and jump in his Father's arms. What a joy it is to laugh and dance, consumed by His love!

When we can be childlike in our hearts we understand that it is okay to feel and express emotion. To cry, laugh and dance all are important ways of expressing what is in your heart for God.

Not Understanding the Human Jesus

We also need to know the human Jesus. We can become so focused on his divinity that we can miss his humanity. In John we read: "There was reclining on Jesus' breast one of his disciples, whom Jesus loved…He, leaning back thus on Jesus' breast" (John 13:23,25). This is a scene we can rush past, but something profound is pictured here. John is getting in touch with Jesus in a way that goes beyond cognitive knowledge. He is leaning his head on the heart of God. "God allows a young Jew, reclining in the rags of his twenty-odd years, to listen to His heartbeat!"[12] In our effort to understand and know God, to read about Jesus and His works, we tragically can overlook the love of Jesus-a love that we "feel" and that testifies "God is Love."

Children look beyond the outer man to see the heart. Childlike faith is not just seeing what Jesus did but understanding His nature, reasons and purpose for His actions.

Jesus came to show us the heart of the Father. And the Father's heart hungers to have time with us-time for us to hear His heartbeat for our lives. This is why spending time with Him is so important. When we wait on Him and minister to Him we can hear and know what is on His heart.

ADOPTED BY GOD

God promises an inheritance to those who come to Jesus as little children. This inheritance is a result of our adoption, which is thoroughly a result of His grace. "He predestined us to be adopted as His sons (children) through Jesus Christ, in accordance with His pleasure and will-to the praise of His glorious grace, which He has freely given us in the One He loves" (Ephesians 1:5). Someone wrote that predestination means that "God has determined beforehand that those who believe in Christ will be adopted into His family and conformed to His Son, but it does not relieve man of his responsibility to believe the Gospel in order to bring to pass God's predestination for him personally."

When adoption is used of believers in the present age, it reveals that at the same moment we become sons or daughters of God we also are adopted by God. Some may know firsthand what adoption means. Ideally when you were adopted you received the same benefits and standing as would a natural child of the family into which you were adopted. Some of you may not know firsthand what adoption means, but you certainly know what privileges you had as a child born naturally into your family.

We have been adopted by God and are likewise sons and daughters of God. We have received the Spirit of adoption. "Because those who are led by the Spirit of God are sons of God. For you did not receive a spirit that makes you a slave again to fear, but you received the Spirit of *sonship* [other translations say *adoption*]. And by Him we cry, 'Abba, Father.' The Spirit Himself testifies with our spirit that we are God's children. Now if we are children, then we are heirs-heirs of God and co-heirs with Christ, if indeed we share in His sufferings in order that we may also share in His glory" (Romans 8:14-17).

Adoption, by its very nature, gives us access to an intimate relationship with God as our "Abba" Father. In this passage from Romans, "Abba" was the word used familiarly by children talking to their fathers. It is a child's word used by children of the Jewish race, a word much like our words *Daddy* or *Papa*.

"What exactly then is the Apostle telling us? The first thing he tells us is that it is a "Spirit of Adoption," by which he means that it is a consciousness of the fact that we have been adopted into the family of God. A consciousness of it, and not merely a belief of the fact. What the Apostle is emphasizing here is that not only must we believe this doctrine and accept it with our minds, but we must also be conscious of it and feel it."[13] God hand picked you, grafted you into His family tree and made you a co-heir with His Son Jesus Christ. All of what He has is yours.

This adoption gives us access to Him, but we also must give Him access to us. When we truly grasp that we are valuable members of God's family and that God loves us as much as he loved Jesus, we will want to hang out with Him just as my granddaughter wants to hang out with my wife and me.

The reality of this love came to me during a healing conference I attended at the Anaheim Vineyard in California in the late 1980s. John Wimber had invited all the pastors to come forward for prayer. We gathered up near the stage and as John prayed I began with deep sobs to sink to my knees. I do not know how long I remained there on my knees, but when I stood up I was flooded with the most incredible warmth of God's love I had ever felt. As I stood there with my eyes closed and my hands raised I asked, "God, how much do you love me?" Immediately I saw in my mind a picture of two hands with the palms open, with deep wounds in them, coming down through the clouds. The moment I realized whose hands they were I felt something touch my open palms and I heard God say, "This much." I was overwhelmed with the depth of God's love for me and wept like a little child, sobbing with joy, unashamed and completely oblivious to those around me.

Scripture declares, "How great is the love the Father has lavished on us" (1 John 3:1). To *lavish* means "to give or bestow in abundance."[14] Have you ever allowed God the Father to love you in this way? Have you allowed Him to so totally pour His love over you that you are overwhelmed and cannot even stand?

COMING AS A LITTLE CHILD

If we are going to come into the Kingdom of heaven we must turn from sin, considering our status or self-importance as insignificant. And we must come with childlike faith and trust. Entrance is by His grace-not by our works. Jesus says in Matthew 19:14, "Let the little children come to me, and do not hinder them, for the Kingdom of heaven belongs to such as these." The Kingdom belongs to those who are trusting, dependent and expectant. As we begin to take on these childlike qualities we will move into a place where we too will want to waste some time with God simply because we enjoy being with him.

8

THE TRAPS OF CONDEMNATION, INTIMIDATION AND ACCUSATION

The enemy uses three traps to keep us under bondage: condemnation, intimidation and accusation. Forgiveness is the key to unlocking and keeping us free of the bondage of these traps. If we are going to deepen our relationship with God and grow in intimacy with Him, we must deal with unforgiveness.

Much of the ground Satan gains in the lives of Christians is due to unforgiveness. Unforgiveness can keep us from moving into intimacy with God because intimacy requires openness, honesty, vulnerability and trust. Vulnerability can be threatening and painful if we have secrets hidden in our hearts. If we are harboring unforgiveness, we effectively can block what God wants to do with us and through us.

WE ARE FORGIVEN!

We must remember we are forgiven! Scripture makes this very clear: "In Him we have redemption through His blood, the forgiveness of sins, in accordance with the riches of God's grace that He lavished on us with all wisdom and understanding" (Ephesians 1:7-8). "For He has rescued us from the dominion of darkness and brought us into the kingdom of the Son He loves, in whom we have redemption, the forgiveness of sins" (Colossians. 1:13-14). Some find it incomprehensible to both understand and accept that they have been forgiven. We may feel that what we have done is so reprehensible that God could never forgive us. Or, we may think that in order to be forgiven and stay in good standing with God, we must prove by our good works, that we deserve to be forgiven.

We have what William Shannon calls "A false and illusory notion of God...(that) sees God as someone who is gracious to me when I am good, but who punishes me relentlessly when I am bad. This is a typical patriarchal notion of God. He is the God of Noah who sees people deep in sin, repents that He made them and resolves to destroy them. He is the God of the desert who sends snakes to bite his people because they murmured against Him. He is the God of David who practically decimates a people, because their king, motivated by pride perhaps, takes up a census of his empire. He is the God who exacts the last drop of blood from his Son, so that His just anger, evoked by sin, may be appeased. This God whose moods alternate between graciousness and fierce anger, a God who is still all too familiar to many Christians-is a caricature of the true God. This God does not exist. This is not the God whom Jesus reveals to us. This is not the God whom Jesus called 'Abba.'"[1]

The God that Jesus revealed to us is beautifully illustrated in John 13:23,25. John, the disciple Jesus loved, was leaning back on Jesus' breast. This is a very tender scene. He was not self-conscious or uncomfortable in this place. This was a very human man with his head on the chest of the Son of God. The disciples wanted to be around Jesus. Peter, even after he had betrayed Jesus by denying and then deserting Him, later jumped into the water and swam like crazy to get to Him. We have account after account of the disciples giving up everything to be with Jesus. I doubt that they lived in a continual sinless state, but they were not paralyzed by their past sin. They recognized that Jesus was the Savior of endless love and forgiveness. This scene with John sends a powerful message to us individually and corporately. "The beloved disciple sends a message both to the sinner covered with shame and to the local church tentative and slow to forgive for fear of appearing lax or liberal. The number of people who have fled the church because it is too patient or compassionate is negligible; the number who have fled because they find it too unforgiving is tragic."[2]

WE ARE TO FORGIVE

In addition to being forgiven we are to forgive. Forgiving others is not always easy because sometimes those people whom we need to forgive have hurt us deeply.

The Sermon on the Mount has had a revolutionary effect on those who have applied it. "You have heard that it was said, 'Love your neighbor and hate your enemy.' But I tell you: Love your enemies and pray for those who persecute you" (Matthew 5:43-44). This was a radical thought. "Love your enemies and pray for those who persecute you!" Our natural response to such a concept is, "What, you want me to love my enemies? That's nuts! These are the people who are out to hurt me! It is their fault I am in this mess!"

It is easy for us to point fingers, to hold onto the wrongs committed against us. We may feel we have a "right" to be angry. What was done to us was wrong and, therefore, it is unfair to forgive so easily. It lets them "off the hook" too easily.

But Scripture is clear that forgiveness is vital to our Christian walk. "Bear with each other and forgive whatever grievances you may have against one another. Forgive as the Lord forgave you" (Colossians 3:13). "Be kind and compassionate to one another, forgiving each other, just as in Christ God forgave you" (Ephesians 4:32).

Most of the ground Satan gains in the lives of Christians is due to unforgiveness. Someone said, "I will never allow another person to ruin my life by making me hate them." When we are angry or bitter because of what someone has done to us, we are the ones who are affected by the emotional turmoil. We drag these harmful emotions around with us like excess baggage. Often times, the person who is responsible is not affected in any way and may not even be aware that he or she has hurt us.

I vividly remember being hurt by a man who was a close friend. I know he was not aware of having hurt me by what he did, and I felt it was not something he would understand if I talked to him about what he had done. I rationalized in my mind that it was not that big of a deal so just forgive him and get on with your life. I noticed that the next time I was around him our relationship had changed.

I was beginning to draw back and did not want to be around him. This went on for many months with my believing I had totally forgiven him. While on vacation my wife and I were staying in a beautiful cabin in the mountains. One morning I walked out on the deck, sat down for my morning cup of coffee and turned on my cassette player to listen to some music. The song that started playing was my friend's favorite song. I felt as if I had been hit in the stomach and started deeply sobbing like a baby. God made it very clear to me that I had not forgiven him. I quickly forgave him and asked God to forgive me for holding that anger inside all these months. I knew I was healed from this anger when I saw my friend the next time. Not only was I happy to see him, but I also ran up to him, gave him a hug and told him how much I appreciated him and his friendship. He never did know that he had done anything to hurt me, and I did not feel it was necessary to tell him. Our friendship is restored, and to this day we remain close.

There are two reasons why it is important that we forgive. First, we are warned to forgive so that Satan cannot take advantage of us. "If you forgive anyone, I also forgive him.

And what I have forgiven-if there was anything to forgive-I have forgiven in the sight of Christ for your sake, in order that Satan might not outwit us. For we are not unaware of his schemes" (2 Corinthians. 2:10-11).

Secondly, we are required to forgive!

"For if you forgive men when they sin against you, your heavenly Father will also forgive you. But if you do not forgive men their sins, your Father will not forgive your sins" (Matthew 6:14,15).

"Therefore, the kingdom of heaven is like a king who wanted to settle accounts with his servants. As he began the settlement, a man who owed him ten thousand talents was brought to him. Since he was not able to pay, the master ordered that he and his wife and his children and all that he had be sold to repay the debt. The servant fell on his knees before him. 'Be patient with me,' he begged, 'and I will pay back everything.' The servant's master took pity on him, canceled the debt and let him go. But when that servant went out, he found one of his fellow servants who owed him a hundred denarii. He grabbed him and began to choke him. 'Pay back what you owe me!' he demanded. His fellow servant fell to his knees and begged him, 'Be patient with me, and I will pay you back.' But he refused. Instead, he went off and had the man thrown into prison until he could pay the debt. When the other servants saw what had happened, they were greatly distressed and went and told their master everything that had happened. Then the master called the servant in. 'You wicked servant,' he said, 'I canceled all that debt of yours because you begged me to. Should not you have had mercy on your fellow servant just as I had on you?' In anger his master turned him over to the jailers to be tortured, until he should pay back all he owed. This is how my heavenly Father will treat each of you unless you forgive your brother from your heart" (Matthew 18:23-35).

In this parable the unforgiving servant is handed over to the jailers, or as the King James translation says, "to the tormentors." When we refuse to forgive we can find ourselves in bondage and torment by guilt, shame, anger, fear or bitterness! Unforgiveness is a prison!

Often we also must forgive ourselves. This may mean repenting of our own sinful behaviors, thoughts and attitudes. Sometimes if we have caused a lot of pain and difficulty for ourselves because of our own choices and responses, it is necessary to appropriate the forgiveness of Jesus by forgiving ourselves and releasing our loads of guilt and shame into the flow of His mercy and grace.

I DESERVE CONDEMNATION!

Unforgiveness is sin and brings with it condemnation. *Condemnation* is "to pronounce judgment against or to declare unfit for use."[3] Condemnation is the first of the three traps that Satan uses to try to keep us from having an intimate relationship with God.

Occasionally we encounter people who feel as if what they have done is so bad that God will not forgive them. They feel that they deserve whatever punishment comes. They can accept that they are forgiven but find it extremely difficult to forgive themselves or the people who hurt them. Some feel like the woman caught in the act of adultery.

> "Jesus returned to the Mount of Olives, but early the next morning He was back again at the Temple. A crowd soon gathered, and He sat down and taught them. As He was speaking, the teachers of religious law and Pharisees brought a woman they had caught in the act of adultery. They put her in front of the crowd. 'Teacher,' they said to Jesus, 'this woman was caught in the very act of adultery. The Law of Moses says to stone her. What do you say?' They were trying to trap Him into saying something they could use against Him, but Jesus stooped down and wrote in the dust with His finger. They kept demanding an answer, so He stood up again and said, 'All right, stone her. But let those who have never sinned throw the first stones!' Then He stooped down again and wrote in the dust. When the

*accusers heard this, they slipped away one by one, beginning
with the oldest, until only Jesus was left in the middle of
the crowd with the woman" (John 8:1-11, NLT).*

Obviously, the adulterous woman was being used by the
Pharisees to bait Jesus. She knew her behavior violated the
Law of Moses and that the penalty of adultery was death.
Her accusers were condemning her, and according to the
law they were correct and justified in their condemnation.
What do you think she was feeling while standing there? I
suspect she was feeling afraid, degraded, guilty and ashamed.

After Jesus dealt with her accusers and they left, He turned
His attention to her. "'Where are your accusers? Did not even
one of them condemn you?' 'No, Lord,' she said. And Jesus
said, 'Neither do I. Go and sin no more'" (John 8:10-11, NLT).

Suddenly she was forgiven, free from condemnation. She
no longer faced a death sentence. She was declared not guilty!
Then she was faced with a choice. Just as the Pharisees had
a choice when Jesus challenged them, she had a choice, too.

She could have left this place not able to accept the fact
that she had been forgiven. Understanding that Jesus had
clearly forgiven her but knowing that she deserved the
punishment of death, she might have been so ashamed and
guilty that she could not accept forgiveness. If this were the
case, Satan would find her an easy target. The enemy would
then be able to keep her trapped under condemnation and
not able to comprehend complete, unconditional forgiveness.
He might say, "You really haven't been forgiven. Look at what
you did-do you think God could forgive you and love you
after what you have done?" Satan loves to trap us in
condemnation. If he can keep us thinking this way, he can
keep us away from deep relationship with God, which
prevents us from growing into the person God designed us
to be. We must accept forgiveness in order to move into
intimacy with Him.

The woman's second choice had to do with forgiving and
releasing her accusers. Bitterness over what had just taken
place would have been easy for her to feel. She had been

publicly dragged in front of the religious leaders, then embarrassed and degraded by their accusations. As a result, everyone in the entire village knew about her affair. If she could not forgive her accusers and release them from what they had done to her, bitterness, anger and resentment could have set in and kept her under condemnation.

Condemnation is often brought about because of words spoken to us by people who are significant in our lives. When others say things to us like, "You'll never amount to anything. You'll always be a loser," we feel as if daggers are driven into our hearts. If we believe those people and accept their statements as true, they can be the very words that condemn us to becoming losers and failures.

I often pray with people who heard such words from their fathers, mothers or others in positions of authority. Those words brought condemnation because they believed them and lived as if they were true. They felt unfit for use. "If you hear a teaching and feel as though it were unattainable in your condition, you have only heard half the message. You missed the grace which is always resident in the heart of God's truth. Truth without grace is only half-true. Remember this always: Grace and truth are realized in Jesus Christ (John 1:17). What God's truth demands, His grace will provide."[4] Condemnation is a trap from which we can free ourselves by understanding who we are in Christ and by forgiving those who hurt us!

Satan knows that if he can keep us from understanding that we are forgiven and from realizing who we are in Christ, he can keep us trapped by condemnation. This is one of the traps that will keep us from spending time with God. If we think we are condemned, as Satan would have us believe, then we act like we are condemned and we never experience the lavish love the Father wants to pour out on us because we believe we do not deserve it. If we begin to see God as He is revealed in Jesus, then we will see ourselves as God sees us. He sees us as forgiven, pure, holy and His beloved. This is what we are to become. As Francis Frangipane says, "The ultimate purpose behind revelation is that what we behold, we are to become."[5]

INTIMIDATION CAN KEEP YOU DOWN!

To *intimidate* means, "to fill with fear, to coerce, inhibit or discourage by or as if by threats."[6] The enemy often tries to intimidate those who are committed to Christ, and this is the second of the three traps that he uses to block us from intimacy with God.

Someone told a story about a tourist who was fishing off the Florida coast when his boat capsized. He could swim, but his fear of alligators kept him clinging to the overturned craft. Spotting an old beachcomber standing on the shore, the tourist shouted, "Are there any gators around here?" "Naw," the man hollered back, "they ain't been around for years!" Feeling safe, the tourist started swimming leisurely toward the shore. About halfway there he asked the guy, "How'd you get rid of the gators?" "We didn't do nothin'," the beachcomber said. "The sharks got 'em."

The man was not intimidated until after he jumped in the water and was heading toward his goal of the shore, where it was safe. The same is often true of us. After we are committed to the Lord, the enemy often tries to intimidate us. If he is successful, he has won a great victory.

Intimidation keeps us from honesty with ourselves and with others. Fear of rejection pervades one's whole life. We believe, "If I dare tell you what I am really like you will reject me. If I expose myself I will be abandoned and ridiculed." Brennan Manning says, "Only in a relationship of the deepest intimacy can we allow another person to know us as we truly are. It is difficult enough for us to live with the awareness of our stinginess and shallowness, our anxieties and infidelities, but to disclose our dark secrets to another is intolerably risky. The impostor does not want to come out of hiding. He will grab for the cosmetic kit and put on his pretty face to make himself presentable. Whom can I level with ?

To whom can I bare my soul? Whom dare I tell that I am benevolent and malevolent, chaste and randy, compassionate and vindictive, selfless and selfish, that beneath my brave words lives a frightened child, that I dabble in religion and in pornography, that I have blackened a friend's character, betrayed a trust, violated a confidence, that I am tolerant and thoughtful, a bigot and a blowhard, and that I really hate okra?"[7]

Our enemy has been so successful at backing us into a corner that we not only fear honesty with others, but we hide all our secret sins and vanities from God, which is the height of absurdity. Intimidation keeps us from deep intimacy with anyone and tragically stops us from laying bare our soul to God, which prevents us from receiving forgiveness for those very things that God will use in us to bless others.

ACCUSATION IS DEADLY!

Accusation is bringing charges against someone. We know from Scripture that Satan is the accuser. John writes, "For the accuser has been thrown down to earth-the one who accused our brothers and sisters before our God day and night" (Revelation 12:10, NLT). How often Satan tries to stop or destroy us with accusation! He accuses us before God, and he accuses us to our faces. We hear him say, "Who do you think you are? You are nothing. You are of no value to God. You do not have any power to overcome that sin. You're such a hypocrite. You call yourself a Christian, but how can you be a Christian and do that? How can you feel that way?" This is the third trap that Satan tries to use to block our intimacy with the Father.

Wholeness Ministries was founded in an American Baptist Church. As those of us in the ministry began to be exposed to the model of healing taught by John Wimber at the Vineyard Fellowship in Anaheim, California, we began to explore how to bring this healing ministry into the church. I was trying to learn all I could about healing-attending seminars, reading books and spending time with people in the healing ministry. We began to offer prayer for healing after our services on Sunday mornings and witnessed some significant physical healings. No one was opposed to physical healing, but when we began to explore the areas of inner healing and deliverance, some of the members started to raise questions about what we were doing and opposition started. Most of the resistance was due to misunderstanding and fear of the unknown.

In their fear and misunderstanding they accused us of manipulating people, of leaning toward "New Age" and of being unscriptural in our teaching. Our integrity, honesty and motives were called into question. We were asked to appear before a group of members and prove that what we were doing was scriptural. Accusations were made that were taken completely out of context. The people bringing these accusations were our friends, and we were deeply hurt by their charges. I found myself becoming angry and resentful. I could not understand why people would do this to us. I remember sitting by a river complaining to God saying, "God, why is this happening when all I want to do is pray for people! What's the big deal here! All I want is for people to be healed."

These charges resulted in anger that affected our ability to minister to people in our church. We were so focused on the opposition that we were distracted from what God clearly had called us to do. This process began to plant doubts in our minds that maybe what we were doing was wrong. We were worried about having to defend what we did and said, and this began to divide us as a team. The end result was that a large contingent of people left the church. Looking back on this incident we can see how easily Satan used this situation to manipulate, divide and destroy people.

Because of these accusations I had to pray through some unforgiveness issues with people who had hurt me. What I did in granting this forgiveness was pull the ground from under Satan. The very things of which Satan was accusing me-anger, bitterness, etc.-I released to God. If I had allowed him to keep me in this trap Wholeness Ministries very well may have been destroyed.

As a young minister, Satan often accused me because of the unforgiveness I had in my life toward my father. I was 18 when my father died as a result of a beating by some men outside a bar where he occasionally went to drink. He was not what one might consider an alcoholic, but occasionally he would go to a local bar and get drunk.

One night he went out and did not come home, so Mom went looking for him and found him outside a bar sitting in his car. He was seriously injured, so she took him to the hospital where he died a week later. Because there was not enough evidence to bring this case to trial the court dropped the charges against the men who had beaten my father. I felt betrayed by the judicial system. I was angry at the police, sheriff, attorneys and judge. This planted in me seeds of anger and rebellion against any authority. I no longer trusted anyone associated with the legal system.

My anger also was directed toward my father. I reasoned that his death was his own fault because he went to the bar, got drunk, got into the fight and died. If he had stayed away from that bar I would still have a father. At this point in my life I needed a father badly and felt abandoned and lonely without him. I was angry with him and angry with God. "How could you let this happen?" I asked. Because I did not want to risk getting hurt again, I would not let God love me deeply or intimately, and I found it difficult to allow other men close relationally. Most of my friendships were superficial.

It was many years before I was able to come to grips with this anger and allow the hurt and pain to surface. When I finally faced the pain, God was able to come in and heal the wounds. Then I could accept God's love and let others get close to me. And after I forgave those involved in this incident, I was able to get on with my life and move into an intimate relationship with God.

As a pastor, I was expected to have an intimate relationship with God, to be open and loving, and to know how to help people develop loving relationships. But I had given the enemy ample ammunition to accuse me, and my hidden anger caused me to pull back from people. Satan stands before God at any opportunity to accuse us, and he takes every opportunity we give him when we hold on to unforgiveness.

To Forgive or Not to Forgive

If we have been trapped by unforgiveness, then we are faced with a decision: to forgive or not to forgive. The decision to forgive causes us to experience freedom and release from sin. Otherwise we remain trapped under condemnation, intimidation and accusation. These traps imprison us. They keep us from spending time with God and from developing a relationship that is rewarding and freeing.

This is not the way life was meant to be lived. "Life is meant to be lived from a Center, a divine Center. Each one of us can live such a life of amazing power and peace and serenity, of integration and confidence and simplified multiplicity, on one condition-that is, if we really want to."[8]

9

WHAT ARE YOU WILLING TO DIE FOR?

The book of Isaiah states clearly God's view of idols and gods: "I am the Lord, and there is no other; apart from me there is no god" (Isaiah 45:5); "Before me no god was formed, nor will there be one after me" (Isaiah 43:10); "All who make idols are nothing, and the things they treasure are worthless. Those who speak up for them are blind; they are ignorant, to their own shame" (Isaiah 44:9).

When we think of idols or idol worship what typically comes to mind are images of people bowing before statues, burning candles and incense or leaving offerings that they hope will please or at least appease the gods. On my trips to India I have witnessed such prevalent idol worship. Idols in many forms are placed on street corners, in shopping malls, in temples and in homes. It is easy to identify idols when they are obvious and an integral part of a culture.

But our American idols are much subtler. For example, we place an inordinate priority on wealth, appearance and education. These things are all good in and of themselves, but in order to obtain them, we spend far too much time in their pursuit. Why? "The pursuit of money, power, glamor, sexual prowess, recognition and status enhances one's self-importance and creates the illusion of success."[1] Almost unconsciously these status symbols become idols that keep us from spending time with God. If we are not careful they become more important than our relationship with God.

OUR CULTURAL IDOLS

It is easy for us to fill our lives with things that become the very idols God wants us to destroy. We all give our time and energy to something. It may be our jobs, families, money and material possessions, status, drugs or alcohol, sex, knowledge, traditions or even other people-but we give our lives to something. The gods and goddesses of the Greek world would be hard pressed to compete with the gods of our world today.

If we examine what is important to us, we likely would admit that idols clutter our lives. Francis Frangipane stated, "An idol is not an occasional sin; it is something that rules us and makes us its slave. For some, fear is an idol; for others it is lust; for others it is rebellion or pride. Whatever challenges Jesus' right to our hearts becomes an enemy to Him, which He will confront."[2]

For example, it is easy to make an idol of the fast paced society about us and thus become its slave. Slaves to this frantic pace will expect everything to happen quickly. Instant messaging through computers and communication via satellite is expected and accepted as the norm.

We expect to be instantly informed. Even with our computers supplying us information faster than we can process it, we are always looking for the newest operating system that promises to make our computers even faster. When we hear of the latest operating system we must have it. We want to immediately dispose of the one we have had for the last three months because it is already old and out of date. Then we must rush out to buy the latest one, which probably will be old and out of date before we unpack it and learn how to use it!

In America we are a busy, driven people. We are driven to succeed in everything! We are busy with our jobs, our families-even our churches! It is easy for us to have our priorities out of order, as there is little in the structure of our culture that encourages us to develop a deep, intimate relationship with God. This is in part because we have lost an appreciation for stillness and solitude but also because it requires obedience.

For some religion is an idol. From lofty intellectual towers we may look down on religious belief systems that we consider primitive, or we may view with disdain churches that adorn their walls with religious statues and images of saints. At the same time we hold tenaciously to an image of God that is in our minds but not in our hearts. If He were in our hearts we would not be in those lofty towers looking down on others. Rather, we would see ourselves as we truly are-down in the mud and muck of life in our tattered rags, looking up, grateful that God has deemed us worthy of redemption. Our "religious knowledge" may pacify us in our anxious striving, but it will not fill our lives with the fullness of God that brings true inner peace. It is good to remember that, "At the day of judgment, we shall not be asked what we have read, but what we have done; not how eloquently we have spoken, but how holily we have lived."[3]

For others, intellectual knowledge can be an idol. We may have an intellectual understanding of God and be quite content with our "God in a box." Regardless of where we live, cultural and doctrinal traditions are ingrained in our minds that determine our image of God. As Blaise Pascal wrote, "God made man in His own image, and man returned the compliment."[4] We think we know God and can therefore love God when He fits our image. But is it possible to love God when we only know about Him? Can we actually "know" a God intellectually without any emotional connection? With our finite minds can we understand the infinite? I cannot comprehend the depths of the ocean or the billions of stars in our galaxy or even the billions of galaxies in the universe. It seems to me that the more we know of God, the more aware we are of how little of God we know.

> *To whom will you compare me or count me equal? To whom will you*
> *liken me that we may be compared? Some pour out gold from their bags*
> *and weigh out silver on the scales; they hire a goldsmith to make it into a god*
> *and they bow down and worship it. They lift it to their shoulders and carry it;*
> *they set it up in its place, and there it stands. From that spot it cannot move.*
> *Though one cries out to it, it does not answer; it cannot save him from his troubles.*
>
> *-Isaiah 46:5-7*

We may assume that God exists and thinks as we do. Our culture, our ethnicity and our definition of sexuality all influence our image of God. But we should really desire to know Him for who He truly is. "Our God is in the heavens; He does whatever He pleases" (Psalms 115:3).

Whatever the idols in our lives, we are foolish to create them and to worship them. Isaiah 44 describes the foolishness of those who make and bow down to idols. The prophet says that the craftsmen who make these idols are mere men, blacksmiths and carpenters who fashion an image from materials God has provided. Part of the wood is used for fire to cook their food or to warm their homes, and from the rest they fashion a god and bow down to worship it. Isaiah wonders how can they be so foolish.

In our lives, what could possibly be so valued that we would sacrifice intimacy with the true God to pursue it? Inevitably, these idols are pursuits that become burdens to us and create a chasm between us and our God.

SHADRACH, MESHACH AND ABEDNEGO

Once we recognize the idols in our culture and in our personal lives, we discover that it is costly to refuse to "worship" them. Daniel 3 gives the account of Shadrach, Meshach and Abednego, three young Israelites, who were captured in a war and brought to Babylon. The Babylonian king, Nebuchadnezzar, had captured Jerusalem and ordered his officials to bring before him young men from the royal family.

These three young Jews had been selected from captivity, picked personally by the king over all the other young men in the kingdom and elevated to positions of authority. Soon after they were chosen to serve King Nebuchadnezzar, the three became known throughout the land as men of intelligence and integrity. They also were well known as men who faithfully worshipped their God.

But they were outsiders-men from a group of captive slaves! Because these outsiders held such high positions in the kingdom, some of the leaders in Babylon set up an elaborate plan to discredit them before the king.

Daniel 3:1-7 shows clearly the opposition to their faith in God. The governors, treasurers, advisors and religious leaders envied Shadrach, Meshach and Abednego and were jealous of the favor the king showed to them. At some point during his reign King Nebuchadnezzar had his craftsmen build an idolatrous image. This image was ninety feet tall, made of gold and possibly fashioned in the image of Nebuchadnezzar-it was customary for the Assyrian kings to erect statues of themselves. The king summoned all his officials and said to them, "When you hear the music, fall down and worship the image I have built."

The building of this image and the command of the king was a blatant "in your face" clash with the belief of these three Jews. When they were brought before the king and commanded to fall down and worship the idol they replied that they were willing to die rather than worship an idol of gold. Even standing in front of a blazing furnace, they made a conscious choice not to compromise their belief in God!

Soon after everyone else had bowed down before the golden image, the astrologers came and said to the king, "These Jews are not doing what you said we all have to do." Notice they referred to them as Jews, stressing the fact that they were foreigners and implying that they would not be loyal. Then they reminded the king that he honored these Jews, implying that the three men lacked gratitude.

After Nebuchadnezzar heard of their refusal to bow down and worship the idol, he was furious with rage. Why would Nebuchadnezzar be so angry? Obviously he was convinced that the king should be obeyed and that no one should dare to challenge his authority! His position was, "After all I have done for you, how could you do this to me!"

But even so, the king gave them another opportunity to bow down. Why would he even bother to give the three a second chance? Most likely because he liked them and did not want to throw them into the furnace. If he were talking to them today the conversation might sound something like this: "Look, I know you are believers in the Hebrew God and I really respect that and want to stay on good terms with you, but there's just this one thing that you've got to do, because if you do not it makes me look bad. If I let you get away with this, then anybody else can challenge my authority." But they still refused to compromise their faith.

Of course, we know the rest of the story:

> Then Nebuchadnezzar was so filled with rage against Shadrach, Meshach and Abednego that his face was distorted. He ordered the furnace heated up seven times more than was customary, and ordered some of the strongest guards in his army to bind Shadrach, Meshach, and Abednego and to throw them into the furnace of blazing fire. So the men were bound, still wearing their tunics, their trousers, their hats, and their other garments, and they were thrown into the furnace of blazing fire. Because the king's command was urgent and the furnace was so overheated, the raging flames killed the men who lifted Shadrach, Meshach, and Abednego. But the three men, Shadrach, Meshach, and Abednego, fell down, bound, into the furnace of blazing fire. Then King Nebuchadnezzar was astonished and rose up quickly. He said to his counselors, "Was it not three men that we threw bound into the fire?" They answered the king, "True, O king." He replied, "But I see

four men unbound, walking in the middle of the fire, and they are not hurt; and the fourth has the appearance of a god." Nebuchadnezzar then approached the door of the furnace of blazing fire and said, "Shadrach, Meshach, and Abednego, servants of the Most High God, come out! Come here!" So Shadrach, Meshach, and Abednego came out from the fire. And the satraps, the prefects, the governors, and the king's counselors gathered together and saw that the fire had not had any power over the bodies of those men; the hair of their heads was not singed, their tunics were not harmed, and not even the smell of fire came from them. Nebuchadnezzar said, "Blessed be the God of Shadrach, Meshach, and Abednego, who has sent his angel and delivered his servants who trusted in him. They disobeyed the king's command and yielded up their bodies rather than serve and worship any god except their own God. Therefore I make a decree: Any people, nation, or language that utters blasphemy against the God of Shadrach, Meshach, and Abednego shall be torn limb from limb, and their houses laid in ruins; for there is no other god who is able to deliver in this way." Then the king promoted Shadrach, Meshach, and Abednego in the province of Babylon.

Daniel 3:19-30

This remarkable story is about faith and trust. It shows that developing a relationship with God can be costly. In this case that cost could have been their lives. These three men were able not only to totally trust God, but they also were willing to die for what they believed. The result was that their faith proved to a whole nation that the God of Israel is the one true God.

It is also about obedience. In America obedience is not something to which we easily adapt. "For the life of obedience is a holy life, a separated life, a renounced life, cut off from worldly compromises, distinct, heaven-dedicated in the midst of men, stainless as the snows upon the mountaintops."[5] Shadrach, Meshach and Abednego were obedient even to the point of death.

One of the obvious things displayed in this account is opposition. It does not take much discernment to see that our culture opposes our beliefs. Christians are often portrayed as bigots, self-righteous, weak and hypocritical.

In the face of such opposition, Shadrach, Meshach and Abednego were confronted with two temptations-the same two temptations we face today. The first temptation was perversion, an attempt to direct them away from what is right. The culture, led by the king, believed that if it could distract the men from God by bowing down before an idol, then it easily could pervert their belief in their God. That is what idolatry is: a perversion of a desire to see God.

The second temptation was to compromise their faith. These three Jews were in positions of power in King Nebuchadnezzar political structure. If they were going to maintain their positions and advance in their profession, they would have to compromise.

It is obvious that nobody else was bothered about bowing down before the idol. Everybody fell down to worship (verse 7). John Maxwell says, "Sometimes a majority means that all the fools are on the same side!"[6]

It is doubtful they fell down because they loved the King. Most likely, they fell down because they were afraid and they knew that if they did not worship this idol they would die! Also, they did not have the conviction or the chutzpah to stand for what they believed. Sometimes it is easy to compromise, to start with what seems to be an insignificant compromise in our integrity or morality. We think, "It is not that big of deal, no one will notice or be hurt by this." We may start by overlooking unacceptable language or behavior portrayed in our television shows. Perhaps we do not speak out on issues like abortion, gay rights or prayer in schools for fear of offending others. But whatever form it takes, compromise eventually costs us relationship with God.

These men were demonstrating with their actions that they believed what they spoke with their mouths. They acknowledged the truth of the accusation and, rather than defend themselves, were willing to rest their case in the hands of God. There was no need to defend themselves. They had full confidence and knowledge in their faith. When they responded this way, they knew God was able to deliver them from the king, but they did not know if God would. Dead or alive, they knew they were in God's hands.

Their understanding of the nature of God led to a fear and awe of Him that caused them to be willing to die rather than serve pagan gods or worship the image of King Nebuchadnezzar. It is difficult to comprehend the depth of their conviction and unshakable faith. Obviously they must have spent a significant amount of time with God to possess these qualities that caused them to face death rather than turn to idolatry. It is also fascinating to find that the proof of the power of their God was not demonstrated until after they were tossed into the fire.

If I were standing in their place looking at that furnace, I am not sure I would be able to do what they did. Have you ever been in a situation where you knew God was able to rescue you, but you were not sure He would? Were you willing to go on regardless of the cost?

We may spend years walking with God, increasing in knowledge and growing into a deep, rich relationship, before our faith is tested. But when the test comes, because of our relationship with the Lord we can stand strong, unwavering even in the face of insurmountable odds.

The miraculous deliverance of Shadrach, Meshach and Abednego from the fiery furnace was designed to show the sovereignty of the true God over the nation that had taken Israel captive. This story is both a victory and a powerful demonstration of the faith of these three men. They were loosed, then protected, God was glorified and they were rewarded. It was a demonstration of their complete surrender to and unwavering trust in God.

"Surrender your poverty and acknowledge your nothingness to the Lord. Whether you understand it or not, God loves you, is present in you, lives in you, dwells in you, calls you, saves you and offers you an understanding and compassion that are like nothing you have ever found in a book or heard in a sermon."[7]

WE MUST DIE TO OUR IDOLS

Anything that stands between us and a deep, intimate walk with God cannot be politely tolerated. We have a jealous God. "You shall not worship any other god, for the Lord whose name is Jealous, is a jealous God" (Exodus. 34:14)! This is not petty, possessive and insecure human jealousy. God's jealousy is based on His pure love for us and His desire to bless us and fulfill our lives in Him. Rather than being simply a philosophical principal of "higher cosmic consciousness," He is a living, loving God who wants to be with us. Richard Foster wrote, "Today the heart of God is an open wound of love. He aches over our distance and preoccupation. He mourns that we do not draw near to Him. He grieves that we have forgotten Him. He weeps over our obsession with muchness and manyness. He longs for our presence."[8]

We must be willing to die to those values that have first place in our hearts. Modern idols keep us from spending time with God and tempt us to perversion, compromise and doubt in God's ability to protect and provide. Though we may not always understand Him or know the outcome of what He does, we must come to the point where we know that "He is able." If we are not there in our walk with Him, then we likely have some "idols" that have replaced Him in our lives.

In his book *Abba's Child*, Brennan Manning makes the case that we are all "impostors." Fearing that people will discover who we really are and will not like us, we hide our real selves. Pride drives us to pretend we are smart when we are around the well educated. Around the wealthy, we pretend we are rich. With "the religious folks," we pretend to be religious. We put on a happy face, pretending we are all together and life is wonderful, when inside we are emotionally imploding. We carry this "impostor" mentality a step further and even let it invade our relationship with God. "The pursuit of money, power, glamour, sexual prowess, recognition and status enhances one's self-importance and creates the illusion of success."[9] This facade can keep us from honesty and transparency, and we may end up merely jumping through religious hoops. All of these imposter motives are actually idols that separate us from knowing God.

And we do not want to just know God intellectually. We must allow Him to move from our heads to our hearts. "To seek our divinity merely in books and writings is to seek the living among the dead; we do but in vain many times seek God in these, where His truth too often is not so much enshrined as entombed. Our theology of God has replaced an encounter with God, and in our hearts there is no one there"[10] To allow anything-especially any idols-to keep us from time with God is to miss the very reason God created us.

10

THE KIND OF PERSON GOD USES

Perhaps you have heard the statement, "I just want to be used by God." Many people flippantly say this without understanding what it is going to cost or considering whether they are willing to pay the price. In order to be the kind of person God uses, we must be willing to spend significant time with Him, and we must understand that this time spent with Him will result in life changes.

The kind of person God uses can best be summarized this way:

- His life objective is to seek first the Kingdom (Matthew 6:33).
- He is willing to pay any price for God's will to be fulfilled in his life (2 Timothy 2:3-6).
- He has a love for God's word (Jeremiah 15:16).
- He has a servant's heart (Matthew 20:26-28).
- He does not have an independent spirit (Ephesians 2:19-21).
- He puts no confidence in the flesh (Romans 7:18).
- He has a love for people (John 15:12).

- He does not allow himself to become trapped in bitterness (Hebrews 12:15).
- He has learned to discipline his life (1 Corinthians 9:24-27).

CONFRONTING THE REALITY OF JESUS CHRIST

A.W. Tozer eloquently says, "Plain horse sense ought to tell us that anything that makes no change in the man who professes it makes no difference to God either, and it is an easily observable fact that for countless numbers of persons the change from no-faith to faith makes no actual difference in the life."[1]

A relationship with God should result in change. I am not simply talking about another layer of religious information. Rather, I am advocating a lifestyle that brings us into the truth and reality of God. Francis Frangipane writes, "But the reality of God is staggering! Peter did not succumb under the convicting power of "religious knowledge"-he met the reality of Jesus Christ! On the road to Damascus, Paul was not blinded and devastated by a "new doctrine"-he met the reality of Jesus Christ! When John beheld our glorified Lord on Patmos, it was not a "new spiritual insight" that left him slain as a dead man-he beheld Jesus Christ!"[2] When we behold the reality of Christ, our lives will change. We will never want to go back to being what we were before.

It is not a matter of attending a seminar or reading a book. It requires more than a day's work or a simple change in lifestyle. It requires a lifetime. It is a change in both thinking and attitude. It requires that we face who we are and what radical changes in our lives need to be made to bring us to that place where we are totally committed to being the men or women that God can use. If you are willing to embark on this journey, be assured that the rewards are beyond measure.

WHAT IS YOUR LIFE OBJECTIVE?

In the early 1970s, a man whose life objective was to make as much money as possible employed me. Being young and impressionable I was quite enthralled with all the trappings of power and money and was on the fast track to acquiring them. My objective was to become rich and powerful. In conversation with him one day I asked, "William, what do you think about God?" He responded, "I do not need God. I have everything I want-money, power and possessions. What do I need God for? He can't give me anything I don't already have." A few weeks later William died when a plane he was flying crashed into a mountain.

Sometime later I thought about him and our discussion. As I looked around the office at all the trappings of power, I heard God saying to me, "Well, Michael, is this what you want to give your life to acquiring?" I realized at that moment that those things to which I had attached such importance were of little value to me, to my family or to God. This event was the beginning of some radical changes in my life objectives.

For most of us, our job is merely a means to an end. We work to earn money to buy necessities like housing, food and transportation. Occasionally we have a bit left over for luxuries. But what we choose to do for a living must never be our life objective, because it is only temporary! We have to live our lives in the present, but we must keep in mind the eternal. And if we seek Him, He will assume responsibility for meeting every need in our lives.

Paul writes, "And the things which you have heard from me in the presence of many witnesses, these entrust to faithful men, who will be able to teach others also" (2 Timothy 2:2). Paul is speaking to the tremendous potential in the life of one man. He is saying to Timothy, "You teach to faithful men the things that I have taught you, and if they will do likewise this message will multiply beyond your wildest imagination." He is talking about a sacrifice of time, energy, talents, desires, even one's self.

When we embark on the quest to know God, allowing Him to release the individual potential He invested in each of us, our life objectives will change. Those things we thought were important will begin to transform us, and we will experience the wonderful freedom of dependence on God and the freedom from dependence on man. "But seek first His kingdom and His righteousness and all these things will be given to you as well" (Matthew 6:33).

WE MUST BE WILLING TO PAY THE PRICE

This journey must become your passion, but this passion will be costly. It cost Jesus His life. In his book *Abba's Child*, Brennan Manning quotes Johannes B. Metz saying, "The one great passion in Jesus' life was His Father. He carried a secret in His heart that made Him great and lonely." Then Manning responds, "The four evangelists do not spare us the brutal details of the losses Jesus suffered for the sake of integrity, the price He paid for fidelity to His passion, His person and His mission. His own family thought He needed custodial care (Mark 3:21), He was called a glutton and a drunkard (Luke 7:34), the religious leaders suspected a demonic seizure (Mark 3:22), and bystanders called Him some bad names. He was spurned by those He loved, deemed a loser, driven out of town and killed as a criminal."[3]

What are you willing to pay to have the will of God fulfilled in your life? In Timothy we read, "Endure suffering along with me, as a good soldier of Christ Jesus. And as Christ's soldier, do not let yourself become tied up in the affairs of this life, for then you cannot satisfy the One who has enlisted you in His army. Follow the Lord's rules for doing His work, just as an athlete either follows the rules or is disqualified and wins no prize" (2 Timothy 2:3-5, NLT).

Is something coming between you and God? Perhaps some secret sin, habit or desire for position and power? We relate easily to money, for example-how much of it we have and who has control of it. Someone said, "The question is not how much money you have in the bank but rather who has the power to draw on your account"!

All that you value must be held with an open hand. God must be free to do with you and take from you as He pleases.

Your health, your dreams, your goals, even your family must be placed at His disposal. The issue here is trust, and the question is, should you not be able to trust Him with everything if His love for you is perfect? "Which of you, if his son asks for bread, will give him a stone? Or if he asks for a fish, will give him a snake? If you, then, though you are evil, know how to give good gifts to your children, how much more will your Father in heaven give good gifts to those who ask Him" (Matthew 7:9-11).

Matthew chapters 1 and 2 tell the story of Joseph, who was to be the father of Jesus. He was faced with some tough choices. His fiancée, Mary, was pregnant. He knew they had not engaged in sexual relations, and he clearly was not the father of the child. In addition to being embarrassing, this situation was socially unacceptable. God said to Joseph in a dream, "Joseph, I want you to marry Mary." He did. Then, after the child was born God spoke again to Joseph and told him to leave his hometown and go to Egypt. He did. Some time later God told Joseph to return to the land of Israel, not going back to their former home in Bethlehem but instead moving to Nazareth. He did. Each of these decisions was costly for Joseph. But he obviously was willing to obey God immediately and protect what God had given him to protect. He was willing to pay any price to have the will of God fulfilled in his life.

If Joseph had not followed God's instructions, the will of God for mankind could have been altered. Joseph's willingness to pay the costly price in his own life enabled God to bring the salvation of mankind to all of us. And it allowed Joseph to serve as the earthly Father of God's Son, the only man in all history to be honored with such a duty. Joseph's priority was in the right place. He focused not on what seemed best to him but, rather, on what God wanted for His life. His relationship with the Father came first. When our highest priority is our relationship with God, the temptations of the world and the wiles of the enemy are much easier to resist, and the will of God can be done in us and through us.

CHANGES ALONG THE JOURNEY

As you spend time with God in your transformation journey, a number of things will happen. These changes will mold you into the person God wants you to be.

Developing A Love for The Word

As you spend time with Him, your love for the Word of God will grow. "Your words are what sustain me. They bring me great joy and are my heart's delight, for I bear your name, O Lord God Almighty" (Jeremiah 15:16, NLT).

Do you have an appetite for the word of God, or do you just snack on it occasionally? I read somewhere that St. Jerome said, "The Scriptures are shallow enough for a babe to come and drink without fear of drowning, and deep enough for theologians to swim in without ever touching bottom."

We really have only one book we must master-the Word of God. Why is it so important for us to know the Scriptures? The Word of God is truth. In the Bible we read that we are accepted, secure and significant. It clearly states that if we are to know God we must dig deep into the depths of His word. If we are to be Jesus to the world we must know Him intimately. To know Him intimately we must spend time in His word, in prayer and worship. Consider this, would you want a surgeon to operate on you who studied medicine the way you study the Scriptures?

Producing the Heart of a Servant

The time spent with God in your transformation journey also will produce the heart of a servant. "Whoever wants to be a leader among you must be your servant, and whoever wants to be first must become your slave. For even I, the Son of Man, came here not to be served but to serve others, and to give my life as a ransom for many" (Matthew 20:26-28, NLT).

A British army slogan reads, "Before you can learn to lead you must learn to serve." John 13 exemplifies this statement in the story of Jesus washing his disciples feet. Not only did he, the master, serve his disciples in this way, but He even served the unlovable. Imagine Jesus kneeling at the feet of Judas, lovingly washing each foot and looking up into his eyes, knowing that Judas was a liar and was about to betray him to the death! Could you have done this, knowing he was going to betray you? But since Jesus did, how can we do anything less? The example of leadership demonstrated by Jesus is an attitude that manifests itself in action. It is difficult for us to understand the concept of leading by serving, but it is one that God must teach us if He is to use us.

Becoming Part of God's Team

The wisdom of the world tells us, "Do your own thing. Do not let people tell you what to do." The Old Testament speaks of an occasion when every man did what was right in his own eyes (Deuteronomy 12:8). But the work of God is a team effort. There is no room for a Lone Ranger attitude that says; "If it is not done my way, then I am not going to do it at all." Spending time with God will cure you of having an independent spirit.

> *"You are no longer foreigners and aliens, but fellow citizens with God's people and members of God's household, built on the foundation of the apostles and prophets, with Christ Jesus himself as the chief cornerstone. In him the whole building is joined together and rises to become a holy temple in the Lord. And in Him you are being built together to become a dwelling in which God lives by His Spirit"* (Ephesians 2:19-21).

Having an independent spirit is like having a car with two steering wheels. Although the car has tremendous potential, if each wheel is turned in opposite directions the car goes nowhere.

Losing Confidence in the Flesh

Putting a lot of confidence in the flesh is like living your life as though you have no need of God. And such confidence in the flesh gives God opportunity to show you how weak you are without Him. "I know that nothing good dwells in me, that is in my sinful nature. For I have the desire to do what is good, but I cannot carry it out" (Romans 7:18).

Francis Frangipane says, "In time, we discover that all true strength, all true effectiveness-yes, our very holiness itself-begins with discovering our need. We grow weaker, less confident in our abilities. As the outer shell of self-righteousness crumbles, Jesus Himself becomes God's answer to every man who cries for holiness and power in his walk. We may think we have spiritual gifts, we may presume we are holy, we may rejoice with human successes, but until we see Christ and abandon our reliance upon our self-righteousness, all we will ever have, at best, is religion."[4]

Loving People

In John 15:12 we read, "My command is this: love each other as I have loved you." We might reasonably ask, "How did Jesus love His disciples?" It would be safe to say there were no limits on His love. In the gospels He demonstrated this many times over. He was patient when they came to Him arguing about who would have the seat next to Him in the coming kingdom. He was encouraging when they were out on the water in the storm and were afraid. He was incredibly trusting and loving even to Judas, His betrayer-many times over He gave Judas opportunities to turn from the path he had chosen. Imagine the kind of love He demonstrated to the woman who was caught in adultery and dragged before the religious leaders to be condemned. Picture the hand of Jesus reaching out to touch the man with leprosy-no one touched lepers!

If we are to love each other like Jesus loves us, we must spend time with Him. We cannot know and feel His heart of compassion and love without being with Him. We cannot give away the kind of love Jesus has if we do not have it for ourselves.

Confronting Sin and Bitterness

When you spend time with God, He will bring to your remembrance areas of anger or bitterness that He wants you to face. He will require that you make peace with all men. He will require that you allow no sin to go unchallenged. "Make every effort to live in peace with all men and to be holy; without holiness no one will see the Lord. See to it that no one misses the grace of God and that no bitter root grows up to cause trouble and defile many" (Hebrews 12:14-15).

In Scripture we are commanded to confront sin when we see it. This is especially true of the sin in our own lives. For instance, if the sin of resentment is left unchallenged it can turn into bitterness. Have you ever noticed that when you are angry with someone, quite often you are the only one who hurts?

Seeking Discipline

On this journey discipline will become an important part of your life.

"Remember that in a race everyone runs, but only one person gets the prize. You also must run in such a way that you will win. All athletes practice strict self-control. They do it to win a prize that will fade away, but we do it for an eternal prize. So I run straight to the goal with purpose in every step. I am not like a boxer who misses his punches. I discipline my body like an athlete, training it to do what it should, otherwise, I fear that after preaching to others I myself might be disqualified" (1 Corinthians 9:24-27, NLT).

We operate under the false assumption that if God wants us to build a relationship with Him, give up a harmful habit or complete a work for Him He will have to give us the strength to do it. Guess what? He already has! It is available. We must simply have the discipline to appropriate it!

If a football player said to his coach: "I'll be out Wednesday to practice, but I am not sure I can come more often than that because I have some important things to do," what kind of a player would he be? In a short time he would not be a player at all. He would be off the team. He's not going to progress beyond where he is because he is unwilling to discipline himself. Likewise, we do not grow in the Lord just because we have become Christians.

At a boys school a new headmaster was chosen from among members of the faculty. After the appointment was announced, a teacher approached the chairman of the selection committee with a gnawing question. "I accept the fact that I was not picked for the headmastership," he said, "but can you tell me why I was not at least considered for the post? It seems curious. After all, I have had twenty years teaching experience here." "That's not quite the way we looked at it," came the reply. "In your case, the board felt that what you've had is one year's experience repeated 20 times."

Do not blame God for your failures when He has already provided a way for you to overcome them. If you are going to be the kind of person God uses, you have to learn to discipline your life. One does not become useful to God by being a weekend Christian.

You see, the gold medal goes to the athlete who has worked hard, who has learned how to discipline himself, who has learned to say no to the many distractions around him, who has a clear cut objective and has resolved to stay with it. This is the kind of person God uses.

OUR FOUNDATION IS CHRIST

At this point you may be saying to yourself, "Hey, I am pretty useful to God. I am a Christian, I go to church, I pay my tithe, and I give a little time now and then to help out with church work. Everything is good, right? Wrong!

"No one can lay any foundation other than the one already laid, which is Jesus Christ. If any man builds on this foundation using gold, silver, costly stones, wood, hay or straw, his work will be shown for what it is, because the day will bring it to light. It will be revealed with fire, and the fire will test the quality of each man's work. If what he has built survives, he will receive his reward. If it is burned up, he will suffer loss; he himself will be saved, but only as one escaping through the flames" (1 Corinthians 3:11-15).

What are you going to do when you stand in front of Jesus, looking into that loving face, with your hands full of ashes because you built your entire life on a foundation of wood, hay and straw? Knowing what He did for you, how are you possibly going to be able to say, "I did not know, I did not have time, or I did not understand"? What if He were to say to you, "Let me take you into this room and show you what your life could have been like if only you had done what I asked, if only you had been faithful to Me, if only you had disciplined your life and made it really count, as I wanted you to do."

The foundation for everything we do is Christ. We build on that foundation because what we build on it is all that matters in the eternal plan of God. "He is truly great, who is great in the love of God. He is truly great, who is humble in mind, and regards earth's highest honours as nothing. He is truly wise who counts all earthly things as dung, in order that he may win Christ, and he is truly learned, who renounces his own will for the will of God."[5]

WE ARE THE TREASURE!

"The Kingdom of heaven is like treasure hidden in a field. When a man found it, he hid it again, and then in his joy went and sold all he had and bought that field" (Matthew 13:44-46).This parable from Matthew is drenched with meaning. To Jesus, we are everything. No cost is too high. Even the suffering, shame and agony of Calvary were worth it to Him.

Lloyd Ogilvie's book, *Autobiography of God,* paints an engaging narrative of this parable:

> *We can feel the emotions of the plowman working the field. He had plowed it many times before. Feel the hot sun beating down, the sweat rolling off his brow, the weary hands gripping the slivered plow handles. Sameness, demanding*

labor, monotony. Then suddenly the plow hits an obstruction. Another rock to be dug out and carried to the side of the field! He got down on his knees and began to dig with his hands. Clump and clod were removed. The hard earth resisted movement. Then the man's hand broke through and he touched the obstruction. Not granite, but the top edge of a chest! The man's heart began to beat faster. Could it be? He knew that treasures were often hidden in the ground. There were no banks. People resorted to the earth to hide their valuables. When war or calamity drove them off their land they would bury their treasures, hoping to return to claim them.

Trembling he yanks open the chest. He is stunned. He lets out a scream that makes the ox blink. The heavy chest is filled to the rim with coins, jewels, silver and gold. He sifts through the treasure, letting the precious coins, the rare earrings and sparkling diamonds slip through his fingers.

Carefully, the peasant looks around to see if anyone has been watching him. Satisfied that he is alone, he heaps the dirt over the chest, plows a shallow furrow over the surface, lays a large stone at the spot as a marker and resumes plowing the field.

He is deeply affected by his splendid find. A single thought absorbs him; in fact, it so controls him that he can no longer work undistracted by day or sleep undisturbed by night. The field must become his property! As a day laborer it is impossible for him to take possession of the buried treasure. Where can he get the money to buy the field? Caution and discretion fly out the window. He sells everything he owns. He gets a fair price for his hut and the few sheep he has acquired. He turns to relatives, friends and acquaintances and borrows significant sums. The owner of the field is delighted with the fancy price offered by the purchaser and sells to the peasant without a second thought. The peasant's wife is beside herself. His sons are miserable. His friends reproach him. His neighbors wag their heads: "He stayed out too long in the sun." Still, they are baffled by his tremendous energy. The peasant remains unruffled, even joyful, in the face of widespread opposition. He knows he has stumbled on an extraordinarily profitable transaction and rejoices at the thought of the payoff. The treasure, which apparently had been buried in the field for security before the last war and whose owner had not survived, returns a hundredfold on the price he had paid. He pays off all his debts and builds the equivalent of a mansion in Malibu. The lowly peasant is now a man whose fortune is made, envied by his enemies, congratulated by his friends and secure for the rest of his life.[6]

What Jesus wants us to realize is that we are His inheritance. We are the treasure! He has given His all for us to have relationship with Him now and to eventually live in heaven with Him for all eternity. Only when we are with Him in heaven will we understand what riches and gain He has hidden from us while we are here on earth. Like the peasant opening the treasure chest, we will be stunned. Many of us do not see ourselves as people of value. We do not understand and cannot comprehend why Jesus would give up His place with the Father to come and spend 33 years with us.

Thirty-three years! Those years were filled with temptation, suffering and death. From the world's perspective these years were a failure, and if we do not grasp that we are God's treasure, then we ourselves also see them as years of failure. If we can accept who we are as chosen people, then we easily can choose to do the Lord's will. "Be imitators of God, therefore, as dearly loved children and live a life of love, just as Christ loved us and gave himself up for us as a fragrant offering and sacrifice to God" (Ephesians 5:1,2).

When we spend prolonged periods in prayer and solitude with Him, then we begin to understand that we are God's treasure. When we begin to grasp that we are significant, accepted and secure, then we will surrender our hearts totally to Him. And when Jesus reigns in our hearts, His will becomes the passionate purpose of our lives. Our pleasures, plans, priorities and popularity must be surrendered.

Imagine what life could be if it was filled with Him and motivated by His love. "When we realize we are the treasure for whom Christ died, we will treasure doing His will at all costs!"[7]

11

Our Goal is Intimacy

I t has been said that to worship is to turn toward and kiss the face of God. Our goal in worship is intimacy with God.

John Wimber defines intimacy as "belonging to or revealing one's deepest nature to another, and it is marked by close association, presence and contact."[1] Webster defines worship as "reverence tendered a divine being or supernatural power."[2] A. W. Tozer says, "Worship means to feel in the heart; that's first-feel it in the heart."[3]

The journey that has brought me to where I am now in my relationship with God began with music. I connect easily with God through worship music. I would often lie in bed at night listening to worship music. I found it relaxing and refreshing. For me, this was emotionally, intimately connecting with God. I would grab my cassette player, go back to the bedroom, close the door, put on my headphones and begin to sing along with the music.

Worship expresses tenderness, intimacy and deep love. It is an emotional kind of love that we feel in our innermost being. When we are intimate with someone we feel something. If we do not feel anything, then we are not involved; we may be there physically, but our minds and emotions are elsewhere.

In some churches worship seems to be considered an extracurricular activity. We tolerate the worship time in anticipation of the sermon when we expect to get the real meat of Scripture, which we believe is the only thing that will help us grow in our relationship with God. We may think that the more we know about God, the more we know God. This is a distorted understanding of relationship. You can know a great amount of information about someone but not know him or her as a person. I can know vast amounts of technical information about flying an airplane, but until I get into the cockpit of a plane and try to fly it I do not really know what it means to fly an airplane. So it is with worship.

Due to my early childhood experiences, worship to me was singing hymns from our old hymnal that seemed to go endlessly verse after verse after verse. The words were strange and made no sense to my young mind. For example, I never could figure out what "a bulwark never failing" actually meant.[4]

During the early 1980s we began to sing what were described as contemporary praise choruses. But again, they did not connect me with God. I vividly remember the first time I walked into the Vineyard Church in Anaheim, California. They were gathered in a large warehouse that had been converted into a meeting place for their church. About two thousand people were present, and they were singing music that reached out and grabbed my spirit the moment I walked in the door. It was praise and worship like nothing I had ever heard or experienced before. My spirit soared as I entered into this worship. The interesting thing was that it came so naturally. I did not have to be taught how to worship. I discovered there was a difference between singing songs about God and singing songs to God. For me, this was a profound revelation that changed my life forever.

Rituals, forms, techniques and methods cannot produce worship. They can assist us in our worship, but when God touches and frees our spirits we can truly enter into worship. "To worship is to experience Reality, to touch Life. It is to know, to feel, to experience the resurrected Christ in the midst of the gathered community. It is breaking into the shekinah of God, or better yet, being invaded by the shekinah of God."[5]

Our goal in worship is not simply to sing songs to Him. Our goal is to know Him better through worship, to touch Him, to be consumed by His Presence. True worship achieves intimacy with our Father.

CREATED FOR A PURPOSE

God created all things for a purpose. "He created the flowers, for instance, to be beautiful; He created birds to sing; He created the trees to bear fruit and the beasts to feed and clothe mankind."[6] And He created human beings to worship Him. We were made for worship! "Shout with joy to God, all the earth! Sing the glory of His name; make His praise glorious" (Psalms 66:1-2).

All of creation worships God, for all creation was made to worship God. Psalms describes the sun, moon, mountains, trees, wild animals, birds, even the snow and the clouds as worshipping God:

> *Praise the LORD. Praise the LORD from the heavens, praise him in the heights above. Praise him, all his angels; praise him, all his heavenly hosts. Praise him, sun and moon; praise him, all you shining stars. Praise him, you highest heavens and you waters above the skies.*
>
> *Let them praise the name of the LORD, for he commanded, and they were created. He set them in place forever and ever; he gave a decree that will never pass away. Praise the LORD from the earth, you great sea creatures and all ocean depths, lightning and hail, snow and clouds, stormy winds that do his bidding, you mountains and all hills, fruit trees and all cedars, wild animals and all cattle, small creatures and flying birds, kings of the earth and all nations, you princes and all rulers on earth, young men and maidens, old men and children.*
>
> *-Psalm 148:1-12*

A.W. Tozer says, "All else fulfills its design; flowers are still fragrant and lilies are still beautiful, and the bees still search for nectar amongst the flowers; the birds still sing with their thousand-voice choir on a summer's day, and the sun and the moon and the stars all move on their rounds doing the will of God."[7] But where is man in all of this?

At the Fall man forfeited his position. As a result we do not worship in the way God meant for us to worship. We have created numerous ideas, books and styles of worship in an attempt to reach that place of worship where we were intended to be. We have come up with changes and adaptations in worship to replace what God originally designed. But all of these fall short of bringing us back to the place of simplicity in our worship that God intended-the place where we once again worship in the way He planned.

We have lost our way. We have come to think that worship is for us. We consistently ask, "What do I get out of it? How does it make me feel?" We describe worship in terms of what we receive from it, not fully understanding that worship is not about us. It is about God. Much of our worship has become a performance that is rooted in fear and pride.

And yet God yearns for us to worship Him, because He wants so badly for us to be restored to that place of intimate communion. Just as He sought out Adam and Eve in the Garden for fellowship, God makes continuous efforts today to initiate, restore and maintain fellowship with us. We should respond in worship when the Spirit of God touches our spirits.

In order to come closer to that place that God created us to be, in order to more fully understand the nature of an intimate relationship with our Creator, we must learn what it means to worship.

Spirit to Spirit

When Jesus was speaking with the Samaritan woman at the well, rather than get caught up in discussing the where and how of worship, He cut across all that and simply said, "We must worship in spirit and in truth" (John 4:19-24). Like the woman, we may be asking a where and how question, while God is concerned that we know what true worship is.

Deep inside every one of us dwells the essence of our being. This entity is our spirit. It is the sum total of who we are. What makes each of us unique is our spirit. We may be from the same cultural background, raised in the same family, have characteristics similar to our brothers and sisters, or even be a twin; but our spirit identifies us as unique. "For who among men knows the thoughts of a man except the man's spirit within him? In the same way no one knows the thoughts of God except the Spirit of God" (1 Corinthians 2:11).

The fact that our personal spirits are what make each of us unique is an important concept in terms of worship. A.W. Tozer says, "As God's self-knowledge lies in the eternal Spirit, so man's self-knowledge is by his own spirit, and his knowledge of God is by the direct impression of the Spirit of God upon the spirit of man. The importance of this cannot be overestimated as we think and study and pray. It reveals the essential spirituality of mankind. It denies that man is a creature having a spirit and declares that he is a spirit having a body. That which makes him a human being is not his body but his spirit, in which the image of God originally lay."[8] This is truly liberating when we read John 4, which says, "But the time is coming and is already here when true worshippers will worship the Father in spirit and in truth. The Father is looking for anyone who will worship Him that way" (John 4:23).

Understanding that the uniqueness of who we are is our spirit, imagine your spirit connected with the Spirit of God while involved in worship of God. "Here the nature of worship is shown to be wholly spiritual. True religion is removed from diet and days, from garments and ceremonies, and placed where it belongs-in the union of the spirit of man with the Spirit of God."[9] This is "religion" at its best.

John & Paula Sandford in their book *Healing The Wounded Spirit* say, "We are born with an alive and awake personal spirit. But that spirit needs to be met, welcomed, loved and nurtured through warm physical affection. If a baby growing from infanthood into childhood does not receive enough human touch, to that degree his spirit is not kept awake nor drawn forth into full functioning ability."[10] They identify this condition as a spirit that is slumbering, or has fallen asleep.

This condition can result in feeling spiritually disconnected from God. You feel like you are just going through the motions. Your sense of God may be that He is alive and loving, but far off and unconnected to you. You may find it impossible to feel emotionally attached to Him.

Perhaps when you are in church and everybody around you is caught up in the incredible worship and praise, you do not feel anything, but rather you wonder how much longer this worship is going to go on. For you, the God of the Scriptures is distant, judgmental or uncaring about you personally.

The Sandfords say that there are two kinds of slumbering spirits. "There are those who never have been drawn forth to life, who early in infancy have fallen asleep and can no longer function. Secondly, there are those who did receive parental and other nurture and so were awake and functioning spiritually, but turned away from worship services, prayer and affection until their spirits fell asleep. In both, the heart has usually hardened as well."[11] They say that this spiritual condition can be caused by poor nurture or neglect.

It is important to grasp this concept of our personal spirit because of the importance of its role in our lives. In the Sandfords' book, *Waking The Slumbering Spirit,* they write that the functions of our personal spirits in relating to God are to feel His presence in corporate worship and in private devotions-to experience communication with God and receive inspiration from God.[12]

OUR SPIRITS NEED AWAKENING

If you are not able to connect emotionally with God, then your spirit most likely needs to be nurtured and awakened. That nurturing comes through family and friends. When your spirit is fully awakened you can connect emotionally with God and love and cherish what is in another person even more than your own life.

A story about General H. Norman Schwarzkopf in Vietnam demonstrates this quality. "On May 28, 1970, a man was injured by a mine, and Schwarzkopf flew to the man's location. While the helicopter was evacuating the injured soldier, another soldier stepped on a mine, severely injuring his leg. The man thrashed around on the ground, screaming and wailing. That's when everyone realized the first mine had not been a lone booby trap. They were all standing in the middle of a minefield.

"Schwarzkopf believed the injured man could survive and even keep his leg-but only if he stopped flailing around. There was only one thing he could do. He had to go after the man and immobilize him. Schwarzkopf wrote,

> *I started through the minefield, one slow step at a time, staring at the ground, looking for telltale bumps or little prongs sticking up from the dirt. My knees were shaking so hard that each time I took a step, I had to grab my leg and steady it with both hands before I could take another...It seemed like a thousand years before I reached the kid.*

"Then the 240-pound Schwarzkopf, who had been a wrestler at West Point, pinned the wounded man and calmed him down. It saved his life. And with the help of an engineer team, Schwarzkopf got him and the others out of the minefield."[13]

Obviously General Schwarzkopf valued this man more than his own life. He was willing to place himself in danger to save this man's life. When your spirit is fully awake and connected to God's Spirit, each person with whom you interact in some way becomes a person of value to you. They are not just a bother, someone placed there to distract you. They, like you, are a creation of God, valued enough that He would send His Son Jesus to die for them.

Worship is not for the timid and comfortable, for it involves risk! It involves opening ourselves up to living our life in the spirit. It involves change! "If worship does not change us it has not been worship. In worship, resentments melt, and we experience an increased power, compassion and greater desire for obedience. Instead of worship becoming a special high or opiate, or escape, it drives us to respond, 'Here am I, send me' (Isaiah.6:8)."[14]

WE NEED TO BE AVAILABLE

Sometimes we miss the connection with God simply because it does not come in the form we think it should. I do not know the author of this poem, but it speaks volumes to the numerous ways in which God tries to speak to us and how easily we miss hearing Him because we are expecting His answer in a specific way.

GOD ARE YOU THERE?
The young man whispered, "God, speak to me,"
And a meadowlark sang, but the man did not hear.
So the young man yelled, "God, speak to me!"
And the thunder rolled across the sky, but the man did not listen.
Then he looked around and said, "God let me see you,"
And a star shone brightly, but the man did not notice.
And the man shouted, "God show me a miracle!"
And a life was born, but the man did not know.
So the man cried out in despair, "Touch me God,
And let me know you are there!"
Whereupon God reached down and touched him,
But the young man brushed the butterfly away
And walked away unknowingly.

If God is seeking, drawing and persuading us to come to Him, our responsibility is to be available. To be available is to make time to be with God. John Wimber says, "We have made room in our gatherings for special music, special speakers and special events. But we have failed to give time or priority to the activity of worship. We certainly would not be willing to do without the preaching and teaching of the Word. But the fact is, teaching the Word, special events, or simply gathering ourselves together doesn't justify the use of the term 'worship' to describe our services."[15]

No matter how badly you want to develop a relationship with someone, unless the person is available to you, it is not going to happen. Can you imagine what it would be like to try to develop an intimate relationship with someone who was never there, who was always busy? God sent His Son not only to redeem us but also to restore relationship with Him. Therefore, we have a responsibility to be in a place where God can seek, draw and persuade us; to be where we can respond. "The important thing about a man is not where he goes when he is compelled to go, but where he goes when he is free to go where he will."[16] Just as you cannot listen to two people talking at the same time, you cannot listen to the voice of God and the voice of the world.

How often do you go to a place where you can be with God? If we are never in a place where we can respond to God, then we will not have intimacy with Him.

Worshipping in Stillness Before God

If we are going to recover intimacy with God we must spend significant time with God. Singing, dancing, shouting, praying, or reading the Word of God are all worship. But, we must take time for silence and solitude if we are to go to the depths with God. When we wait in quietness before God we begin to feel His heart and know Him intimately.

Waiting is difficult for us because we often view it as a waste of time. We hate to wait for anything. Why is waiting so important? The Psalmist writes, "Find rest, O my soul, in God alone; my hope comes from Him. He alone is my salvation; He is my fortress, I will not be shaken. My salvation and my honor depend on God; He is my mighty rock, my refuge" (Psalm 62:5-7).

This Scripture indicates that in waiting we find rest. Chuck Swindoll says, "Waiting involves trusting. Waiting includes praying. Waiting implies resting."[17]

"When all kinds of trials and temptations crowd into your lives, my brothers, do not resent them as intruders, but welcome them as friends! Realize that they come to test your faith and to produce in you the quality of endurance. But let the process go on until that endurance is fully developed, and you will find you have become men of mature character with the right sort of independence" (James 1:2-4, J.B. Phillips).

"We grow and we learn-not when things come our way instantly, but when we are forced to wait. That's when God tempers and seasons us, making us mellow and mature." [18]

WORSHIP HELPS US TO UNDERSTAND OUR WORTH

Waiting allows me to get in touch with my own belovedness. I cannot connect with others if I am not connected with myself. I cannot be connected with myself if I am not spending time with my Creator, who is the source of my worthiness.

Understanding my value and worth frees me from dependence on other people. "When I allow God to liberate me from unhealthy dependence on people, I listen more attentively, love more unselfishly and am more compassionate and playful. I take myself less seriously, become aware that the breath of the Father is on my face and that my countenance is bright with laughter in the midst of an adventure I thoroughly enjoy." [19]

Conscientiously "wasting" time with God allows us to gain a true perspective on life, and it helps us to know what is of value in nurturing our souls. It allows us to speak and act from strength rather than from fear and insecurity. It helps us to begin to understand and know that God is God. Anthony Padovano commented, "It means I don't figure out and don't analyze, but I simply lose myself in the thought or the experience of just being alive, of merely being in a community of believers, but focusing on the essence or presence rather than on what kind of pragmatic consequences should follow from that, merely that it's good to be there, even if I don't know where 'there' is, or why it's good to be there. Already I have reached a contemplative stillness in my being." [20]

Worship allows you to understand that it is God who has called you by name. "Do not be afraid, for I have redeemed you; I have called you by your name, you are mine. You are precious in my eyes, because you are honored and I love, you...the mountains may depart, the hills be shaken, but my love for you will never leave you, and my covenant of peace with you will never be shaken" (Isaiah 43;I,4; 54:10).

The tender feelings that He has for you are like those of a father whose child is sitting in his lap, whose arms are wrapped lovingly around the child who is resting in complete security and peace, knowing that in this place there is acceptance, protection and love. In this posture you should be able to "continue day by day, and week by week, until you have drawn near enough to God that you can hear His voice, becoming confident that He is close enough to you to hear your whisper."[21]

TRUE WORSHIP

Worship involves the total personality-mind, emotions and will. It is not just something we do to feel good. "And you shall love the Lord your God with all your heart and with all your soul and with all your might" (Deuteronomy 6:5). True worship is not passive, nor is it simply a mood or a feeling. Rather, worship is participative and responsive. It is a declaration of celebration. It is not the mumbling of prayers or hymns or praise choruses with little thought and less heart. It is not simply music done either poorly or as a polished performance. It is not something we do to fill the time until the sermon. True worship celebrates God and brings Him pleasure.

But when we worship we also benefit. For example, when you take someone you love out to dinner for a special evening, you do not normally sit there like a bump on a log, uninvolved in the evening. You are there because you love him or her and you are doing something special for that person. He or she is blessed by your gift, but so are you, because you are participating in a loving act of intimacy.

The life of true worship is a life of surrender. David Wilkerson says, "The surrendered life is the act of giving back to Jesus the life He granted you. It is relinquishing control, rights, power, direction, all the things you do and say. It is totally resigning your life over to His hands, to do with you as He pleases."[22] Understanding this kind of surrender is key to worship. If we are totally surrendered to Him, then our entire lives become lives of worship. Worship is the key to building relationship with God.

Spending time in worship can be different for each of us. You may prefer jubilant singing and dancing accompanied by guitars, drums and clashing symbols. Or worship for you may be singing hymns accompanied by choirs and organ music. You may best worship in quietness and prayer. Or you may prefer each of these worship methods at different times in your walk with the Lord. All are important, and all are acts that bring us closer to God. And God loves it when we participate in each of them.

Whether it is joyfully dancing or kneeling in reverence, worship is our love expressed to God, for God Himself. William Temple said, "To worship is to quicken the conscience by the holiness of God, to feed the mind with the truth of God, to purge the imagination by the beauty of God, to open the heart to the love of God, to devote the will to the purpose of God."[23]

Worship is not a performance; it is an act of intimacy. Worship is my spirit connecting with His Spirit. The very idea that the Creator of the universe would even permit us to come into His presence should fill us with a sense of gratitude, awe and reverence. The God who created the universe, who heals the sick, who knows you need food and shelter to survive, against whom all military might is but a puff of dust and beside whose power a swirling, raging river is but a trickle in the sand-THIS is the God worthy of our worship!

12

The Reality of God

If you were to describe how you feel about your relationship with God, what would you say? This question was posed to me recently. As I thought about my answer, an old hymn came to mind. The hymn is "I Stand Amazed," and it eloquently expresses how I feel:

> *"I stand amazed in the presence of Jesus the Nazarene*
> *And wonder how He could love me, a sinner condemned, unclean.*
> *How marvelous! How wonderful! And my song shall ever be:*
> *How marvelous! How wonderful is my Savior's love for me!"* [1]

I sometimes cannot grasp how God could love me so completely and unconditionally. When I am honest enough to be transparent with Him and myself, when I understand how ugly and sinful I am without Him, I stand amazed. We should be completely amazed that He loves us and forgives us unconditionally. When you think back over your life and what you have done, when you honestly examine yourself and what you think or say or do, do you not stand amazed that He is always there, that He will never leave you or forsake you?

As I continue this journey into the depths with God, I am beginning to grasp with my finite mind that what God is revealing about Himself is absolutely staggering! Pause and think about this for a moment. The God of the Universe is urging, inviting and persuading us to spend time with Him. He is willing to reveal Himself to us and transform and conform us to the image of Jesus Christ. He wants to have relationship with us, and He does this through revealing Jesus Christ to us. Let's not allow ourselves to be distracted by a new layer of religious knowledge, a new doctrine or a new spiritual insight. Let's seek to grasp the reality of God!

A LIFE OF OBEDIENCE

In our relationship with God, I suspect we all want to walk in obedience, to experience holiness, to live a life that is extraordinary in its oneness with the Master. In chapter 5 I quoted Meister Eckhart, who wrote: "There are plenty to follow our Lord halfway, but not the other half. They will give up possessions, friends and honors, but it touches them too closely to disown themselves."[2] What an astonishing thought- a life of complete obedience without any reservations! It seems impossible to even consider how this can be done. Thomas Kelly says this kind of obedience comes when we grasp the vision of the wonder of such a life. As we spend time reading and thinking about the incredible words of Scripture, the stories of God moving throughout history and the accounts of the works of Jesus, we begin to grasp the vision of such a life of complete obedience.

As I consider this life of obedience, what is freeing to me is that it does not depend entirely upon me. In the flesh I cannot achieve it. Rather, it must be a work of the Spirit within me. He is the one who urges, invites, persuades and encourages us in this life of obedience because He knows what a life of wonder and power it is. He is aggressively initiating and seeking relationship with us. He is the One who gives us the power to become children of God. The realization of this is incredibly freeing. I do not have to "suck it up" and tackle this task with all the strength I can muster. In fact, the more I determine to do this in my own strength, the more miserably I fail. "I will do this" is not obedience. Rather, "I will let Him do this in me" is obedience.

Although this life of obedience does not depend entirely on us, it does in part. Our responsibility includes spending time with Him, setting aside all other responsibilities, activities, etc. to simply be with Him. For only in spending time with Him can we achieve the intimacy that He-and we-so desire.

Though the Spirit urges, invites and persuades, we must be in a place both physically and emotionally to recognize His prompting us to deeper relationship with Him. If we are to live lives of obedience we must take seriously the words of Scripture: "Be still and know that I am God" (Psalm 46:10); "Yet those who wait for the Lord will gain new strength; they will mount up with wings like eagles, they will run and not get tired, they will walk and not become weary" (Isaiah 40:31, NAS). To be still, to wait, to give ourselves to God unreservedly may seem a daunting task, but once begun the task soon turns into a journey of adventure and expectancy-a journey that will take us into the presence of our Creator, a place from which we will not easily be pulled. This is what God requires of us.

THE TRAP OF COMPLACENCY

Yet as we pursue our everyday lives, it is so easy to forget Who is calling us into relationship. How easily we put the King of the Universe into our back pockets only to pull Him out when we need Him. How easily the routine of our daily lives blurs the reality of the Most Holy God waiting for us to notice Him. How easily we forget that God desires a genuine, intimate, bottom-of-our-souls relationship with us. How soon we forget that when Jesus answered the disciples' request, "Show us the Father," He said, "If you have seen me, you have seen the Father" (John 14:8-9).

How easy it is to fall into the trap of complacency and familiarity! It is vital that at all times we keep in mind the reality of this God who calls us to Him, and that we are obedient to follow His call.

HE REVEALS HIMSELF

Once we are obedient to be still and be with Him, God reveals Himself to us in an infinite variety of ways. For example, when I simply sit quietly with Him a peace begins to settle over me that stills my busy mind and spirit. Physically I begin to relax and enjoy being still. I know my Father God is there because He speaks to me-not audibly but with thoughts that are whispered in my mind. He tells me how much I am loved and how happy He is to have me there with Him. My spirit is connected to His spirit and is refreshed and renewed. Later, when I read His Word and He reveals more of Himself to me, I experience a freshness about it that surprises and excites me.

But He reveals Himself in other ways, too, such as through the staggering glory of His creation. Whether I am standing and overlooking Niagara Falls, sitting on top of Half-Dome in Yosemite Valley, or standing alongside one of the Giant Redwoods in Sequoia National Park, I am overwhelmed with the enormity and beauty of it all.

And He speaks to me through the creations of others, such as through the written word, a song or beautiful works of art. Whether I am looking at pictures in the Louvre, overcome with emotion by a beautiful piece of music or kicking back beside a raging river, my spirit is connected with God and overwhelmed with His revealing of Himself in such a variety of ways.

It does not matter whether you connect with God through His creation, through the creation of others, or through sitting quietly with Him in an empty room. He will reveal Himself to you in ways that He knows will speak directly to your individual heart. He asks only that you be still long enough to listen.

HE IS SO PROUD OF YOU!

What I have come to understand is that not only is His creation staggering, but the reality of His love also is staggering. It recently struck me that God is proud of me!

It is difficult for us to grasp that God is proud of us. Like a father is proud of his son or daughter, so our Father God is proud of us. We might rightly respond; "What is there to be proud of? I have never done anything significant. I am not famous, I have never written a book or composed a song. I do not paint or write poetry. I do not know how to build anything with my hands, fix the car or grow a garden. All the houseplants my friends give me soon die, though not for lack of trying. What's to be proud of?"

In his book *The Ragamuffin Gospel*, Brennan Manning writes: "Has it crossed your mind that I am proud you accepted the gift of faith I offered you? Proud that you freely chose me, after I had chosen you, as your Friend and Lord? Proud that with all your warts and wrinkles you haven't given up? Proud that you believe in me enough to try again and again?"[3]

Wow, can you get a hold of this? He is looking at you through the eyes of a father looking at his child and saying, "I am so proud of you! You have accepted what I have offered, and you do not give up but keep trying again and again. That is so great! Do you know how it makes me feel that you want me? Do you know how much it means to me to see the hours you spend trying to learn more about me-your singing, praying, sitting quietly just to be with me? Do you know how proud it makes me feel that you *want* to be with me? All the things you could be doing and you chose freely to spend time with me. I know you have sins and struggles. I know that you are not where you feel you need to be for me to love and accept you. But I still love you. And I am proud of you!"

We may not know how to handle the love and pride of a father for whom we do not have to do anything. If you were fortunate enough to grow up in a home with loving parents, then you know that from the time you were born they were proud of you. Proud of your first steps. Proud of those crayon squiggles on paper that were taped up on the walls like Rembrandt paintings. Proud of you when you came running into the room to show them your latest Play-Doh® masterpiece. You knew they accepted you even when you failed again and again. You did not have to prove anything to them. You knew that there was nothing that would keep them from loving you no matter how often you ran from them and hid in your shame and embarrassment. And our Lord loves us even more than our parents.

I remember a time when one of our sons was in the midst of serious rebellion. As his parents we could not stop him from doing those things that we knew could potentially destroy him. But we could love him. During one of those moments he screamed at us in frustration, "The problem is that you love me too much! Why can't you be like my friends' parents who don't care what they do?" He was actually frustrated because no matter what he did we never stopped loving him. That love was causing him guilt and frustration, because it would have been much easier for him to rebel if we had simply rejected him. But we could not do that, and that love eventually paid off.

Your Father God is proud of you because you are His and He quite simply loves you. He understands all of your humanness. Take it into your heart and your soul-Father God is proud of you! Do not try to analyze, understand or "live up" to anything you think will make Him proud because it is not what you do but, rather, what you are. You are His. Believe it, accept it and live in the glorious freedom of it!

Why Not?

If much of your journey with God consists of doing things for Him, then you are missing the best part of the journey. God does not want your doing as much as he wants you. If you are tired of seeking approval in superficial relationships or working to live up to someone else's expectations, then get alone with God and just hang out. If you can stop your pretense and striving for approval long enough to sit quietly with God, then you will find that you are significant, accepted and loved. Regardless of your personal circumstances, your weaknesses and even your sins, God wants to be with you.

He will not love you any more or any less because of what you do or do not do. He will not love you any more tomorrow than he loves you today. He loves you as much as He will ever love you.

He *wants* to be with you. His heart longs for you! Even more than that, He created you so that He could be with you. That is your purpose for being! We are His chosen, set apart, loved ones-and nothing we do can change that.

As you pursue a closer walk with the Lord, as you pursue a life of spending more time with Him, I encourage you to grasp the reality of God and remember who He is. Keep in mind that the King of Kings, the Lord of Lords, our Creator and the Creator of all the universe is offering us the opportunity to spend as much time as we want with Him. We can worship Him, talk to Him, listen to Him and let Him love us. That should cause us to stand amazed.

So why not enjoy the journey? Why not allow yourself permission to just be with Him? Why not claim your place at His side?

Why not waste some time with God!

ENDNOTES

Notes: Chapter 1
Waiting and Wasting

1. Thomas Kelly. *A Testament of Devotion*. San Francisco: Harper Collins, 1992, p. 12. Adapted
2. Dutch Sheets, *Intercessory Prayer*. Ventura: Regal Books, 1996, p.17.
3. Simon & Garfunkel, *Bridge Over Troubled Water*. BMI, 1970.
4. Kelly, p. 89-90.
5. As quoted in Manning, Abba's Child, p. 56.
6. Brennan Manning. *Abba's Child*. Colorado Springs: Navpress, 1994, p. 39.
7. C. Raymond Beran (source unknown).
8. Kelly, p. 1.
9. Lloyd John Ogilvie. *When God First Thought of You*. Waco, Texas: Word, 1978, p. 19.
10. As quoted in Manning, Abba's Child, p. 17.
11. Manning, p. 16.
12. Henri Nouwen. *Life of the Beloved*. New York: Crossroad, 1992, p. 26.
13. Ibid, p.28.
14. As quoted in Manning, Abba's Child, p. 18.

Notes: Chapter 2
The Value of Nurturing the Soul

1. Thomas Kelly, *A Testament of Devotion*. San Francisco: Harper Collins, 1992, p. 96.
2. A..W. Tozer, *The Divine Conquest*. New Jersey: Spire Books, 1950, p.22.
3. David Seamands, *Healing for Damaged Emotions*. Wheaton, Illinois: Victor Books, 1981, p. 49.
4. Dr. Charles Kraft, *I Give You Authority*. Grand Rapids:Chosen Books, 1998, adapted.
5. George A.. Maloney, *Alone With The Alone*. Notre Dame: Ave Maria Press, 1982, p.194.
6. A..W. Tozer, *The Divine Conquest*. New Jersey: Spire Books, 1950, p. 23.
7. Thomas Kempis, *The Imitation of Christ*. New York: Barnes & Noble, 1953, p. 31.
8. John Bradshaw, *Healing The Shame that Binds You*. Deerfield Beach, Florida: Health Communications Inc., 1988, p.66.
9. Kraft, *I Give You Authority*. P.234
10. Neil Anderson, *The Bondage Breaker*. Harvest House, 1990, p. 229-231.
11. Neil Anderson, *Victory Over The Darkness*. Ventura: Regal Books, 1990, adapted from this book's teaching on our identity in Christ.
12. John Maxwell, *Developing The Leader Within You*. Nashville: Thomas Nelson, 1993, p.145-146.
13. Kelly, *A Testament of Devotion*, p. 96.

Notes: Chapter 3
The Benefits of Waiting on God

1. Danny Daniels. *To Be With You*. Anaheim, Calif.: Mercy Publishing, VMI Studios, 1989.
2. Francis Frangipane. *Holiness, Truth and the Presence of God*. Marion, Iowa, 1986, p.101-102.
3. The New American Heritage Dictionary, Third Edition. New York: Dell Publishing, 1994.
4. Richard Foster. *Prayer*. San Francisco: Harper Collins, 1992, p.155.
5. Brennan Manning. *Abba's Child*. Colorado Springs: Navpress, 1994, p.55.
6. Scott Peck. *The Road Less Traveled*. New York: Touchstone, 1980, p.15.
7. Richard Foster. *Prayer*. P. 155

Notes: Chapter 5
The Tragedy of the Church Today

1. A..W. Tozer. *The Root of the Righteous*. Harrisburg: Christian Publications, 1955, pp.61-62 (adapted).
2. Ibid., Tozer, pp.62-63 (adapted).
3. Thomas Kempis. *The Imitation of Christ*. New York: Barnes & Noble, 1993, p.50.
4. A.W. Tozer. *Keys to the Deeper Life*. Grand Rapids: Zondervan, 1957, p.18.
5. Source Unknown-This is a quote by Thomas Merton but I could not locate the source.
6. New American Heritage Dictionary, Third Edition. Dell Publishing, New York. 1994
7. Thomas Kelly, *A Testament of Devotion*. San Francisco: Harper, 1941, p.27
8. A..W. Tozer, *The Divine Quest*. Old Tappan: Spire Books, 1950, p.27.
9. Brennan Manning. *Abba's Child*. Colorado Springs: Navpress, 1994, p.38.
10. Tozer, *Keys to the Deeper Life*, p.28.
11. Ibid, pp. 47-48.
12. Francis Frangipane. *Holiness, Truth and the Presence of God*. Cedar Rapids: Arrow Publications, 1986, p.12.
13. Ibid, p.13.
14. As quoted by Thomas Kelly, *A Testament of Devotion*. San Francisco: Harper, 1941, p.26.
15. Thomas Kempis, *The Imitation of Christ*, p.110.
16. T. Kelly, Ibid. p. 35
17. Read this in a church bulletin at Bakersfield Christian Life Center. The source was not noted.
18. Read this in a church bulletin at Bakersfield Christian Life Center. The source was not noted.
19. Ibid, Manning, p. 141.
20. T. Kelly, Ibid. p. 34

Notes: Chapter 6
The Foolishness of God

1. Webster's Seventh New Collegiate Dictionary, G.&C. Merriam Co. Sprinfield, Mass. 1963.
2. Ibid.

Notes: Chapter 7
When It Is Okay to Be a Child

1. As quoted in Brennan Manning. *Abba's Child*. Colorado Springs: Navpress, 1994, p.89.
2. Lloyd Ogilvie. *Autobiography of God*. Glendale: Regal Books, p.129.
3. Thomas Kelly. *A Testament of Devotion*. San Francisco: Harper Collins, 1941, p.28.
4. Source unknown.
5. Source unknown.
6. As quoted in Manning, Abba's Child, p. 96
7. Manning, p.97.
8. Ibid, p.96
9. As quoted in Manning, Abba's Child, p. 96
10. A. W. Tozer. *The Divine Conquest*. Old Tappan: Spire Books, 1950, p. 30.
11. As quoted in Manning, Abba's Child, p.98
12. Manning, p.124 (adapted).
13. Dr. Martin Lloyd Jones. Romans-Banner of Truth, 1974, p.23
14. The American Heritage Dictionary, Third Edition. New York: Dell Publishing, 1994.

Notes: Chapter 8
The Traps of Condemnation, Intimidation and Accusation

1. As quoted in Brennan Manning. *Abba's Child*. Colorado Springs: Navpress, 1994, p.154.
2. Ibid., p.131.
3. The American Heritage Dictionary, Third Edition. New York: Dell Publishing, 1994.
4. Francis Frangipane. *Holiness, Truth and the Presence of God*. Marion, Iowa: Advancing Church Publication, 1986, p.23.
5. Ibid, p.24.
6. The American Heritage Dictionary, Third Edition. Dell Publishing, New York. 1994.
7. Manning, pp.163-164.
8. Thomas Kelly. *A Testament of Devotion*. San Francisco: HarperCollins, 1941, p.93.

Notes: Chapter 9
What Are You Willing To Die For?

1. Brennan Manning. *Abba's Child*. Colorado Springs: Navpress, 1994, p.31.
2. Francis Frangipane. *Holiness, Truth and The Presence of God*. Cedar Rapids, Iowa: Arrow Publications, 1986, p.71.

3. Thomas Kempis. *The Imitation of Christ*. New York: Barnes & Noble, 1993, p.31.
4. As quoted in Manning. *Abba's Child* p.18
5. Thomas Kelly. *A Testament of Devotion*. San Francisco: HarperCollins, 1992, p.39.
6. Maxwell, John, Source Unknown
7. As quoted in Manning, Abba's Child, p.18.
8. Richard Foster. *Prayer*. San Francisco: Harper, 1992, p.1.
9. Manning, p.31.
10. A. W. Tozer. *The Divine Conquest*. Old Tappan: Spire Books, 1950, p.25.

Notes: Chapter 10
The Kind of Person God Uses

1. A. W. Tozer. *Man: The Dwelling Place of God*. Harrisburg, Penn.: Christian Publications, Inc., 1966, p. 31.
2. Francis Frangipane. *Holiness, Truth and The Presence of God*. Cedar Rapids, Iowa: Arrow Publications, 1986, p.26.
3. Brennan Manning. *Abba's Child*. Colorado Springs: Navpress 1994, p.138.
4. Ibid., Frangipane, p.45-46.
5. Thomas Kempis. *The Imitation of Christ*. New York: Barnes & Noble, 1993, p.32.
6. Lloyd Ogilvie. *Autobiography of God*. Glendale, Calif.: Gospel Light, 1979, p.109 (adapted).
7. Ibid., p.116.

Notes: Chapter 11
Our Goal is Intimacy

1. Wimber, John, This quote was in a sermon heard by the author.
2. Webster's Seventh New Collegiate Dictionary. Springfield, Mass.: G & C Merrian Company, 1963.
3. A. W. Tozer. *Worship, The Missing Jewel of The Evangelical Church*. Harrisburg, Penn.: Christian Publications, 1961, p.8.
4. Luther, Martin. "A Mighty Fortress Is Our God," Paragon Associates, Inc. 1976.
5. Richard Foster. *Celebration of Discipline*. San Francisco: HarperCollins 1998, p.158.
6. A. W. Tozer. *Worship, The Missing Jewel of The Evangelical Church*. Harrisburg, Penn.: Christian Publications, 1961, p.7.
7. Tozer, p.11.
8. A. W. Tozer. *Man: The Dwelling Place of God. Harrisbury, PA: Christian Publications, 1966,* pp.9-10.
9. Tozer, p. 10

10. John & Paula Sandford. *Healing The Wounded Spirit*. Tulsa, Okla.: Victory House, Inc. 1985, p.107.

11. Sanford, p.107.

12. John & Paula Sandford. *Waking The Slumbering Spirit*. Arlington, Texas: Clear Stream Publishing, 1993, adapted pp. 52-58.

13. John Maxwell. *The 21 Indispensable Qualities of a Leader*. Nashville, Tenn.: Thomas Nelson Publishers, 1999, pp.134-135.

14. Ibid., Foster, p.173 (adapted).

15. John Wimber. Worship Seminar. Anaheim, California: Vineyard Ministries.

16. Ibid., Tozer, p. 158

17. Chuck Swindoll. *Three Steps Forward Two Steps Back*. Nashville, Tenn.: Thomas Nelson Publishers, 1980, p.83 (adapted).

18. Swindoll, p.83.

19. Brennan Manning. *Abba's Child*. Colorado Springs: Navpress, 1994, p.56.

20. As quoted in Manning, Abba's Child, p. 57

21. Francis Frangipane. Holiness, Truth and the Presence of God, Cedar Rapids, Iowa: Arrow Publications, 1986, p. 14,15.

22. David Wilkerson. *The Surrendered Life*. Lindale, Texas: World Challenge Inc. Publications, January, 2002.

23. Richard Foster. *Celebration of Discipline*. San Francisco: HarperCollins 1998, p.158.

Notes: Chapter 12
The Reality of God

1. Charles H. Gabriel. "I Stand Amazed." Copyright 1976, by Paragon Associates Inc.

2. As quoted in Thomas Kelly. *A Testament of Devotion*. San Francisco: Harper Collins, 1992, p. 26.

3. Brennan Manning, *The Ragamuffin Gospel*, Sisters, Oregon: Multnomah Publishers Inc. 1990, 2000, p.149.

About Wholeness Ministries

In 1989, Mike Evans founded Wholeness Ministries, a ministry whose two-fold purpose is to pray for healing and to train and equip others to pray for healing. This ministry of healing prayer is based on the mandate of Jesus Christ in Luke 4:18-19. We believe this mandate is to be carried out under the guidance and in the power of the Holy Spirit.

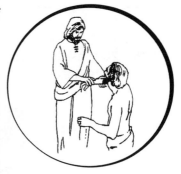

Mike is available for retreats, conferences and workshops. He and his team have taught and ministered extensively in Northern Ireland, England, Puerto Rico, Hungary, India and extensively throughout the United States. To schedule a Wholeness Ministries training conference, or to receive additional information, please contact:

P.O Box 80503
Bakersfield, California 93380 U.S.A
Phone: (661) 833-2920
Fax: (661) 833-2934
E-Mail: mevans@wholeness.org
www.wholeness.org

How to Pray for Others with Tangible Results... the
Learning to Do What Jesus Did
Media Series

Product #40 | Prayer Team Ministry Training Book

In *Learning To Do What Jesus Did*, you will discover unique approaches to praying for others. You will find a step-by-step plan for experiencing the healing power of Jesus in your ministry. After reading this book you will feel a new sense of freedom in praying for others. You will see wonderful, dynamic results as God uses you in exciting new ways to do the things Jesus did. This book will arm you with new knowledge, tools and confidence in praying effectively for yourself and others. As you will discover, learning to pray effectively is learning to follow Jesus.

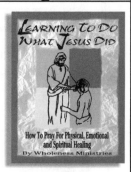

Book • $18 (plus shipping)

Product #41 | 9 Videotape Series

This nine-tape video series is a must for pastors and lay ministers alike. It features approximately 10 hours of teaching from Michael and Jane Evans that will make ministering in the authority and power of Jesus easy to understand and exciting. Mike and Jane have taught this in many different denominations as well as several countries around the world. This series features the following tapes:

1) Introduction to Healing
2) A Healing Model
3) The Role of Faith
4) Authority of the Believer
5) Introduction to Inner Healing
6) Biblical Examples of Inner Healing
7) Forgiveness and Inner Healing
8) Deliverance
9) Spiritual Warfare

9 Valuable VHS Videos • $146 (plus shipping)

Product #42 | 8 Audiotape Series

This eight **audio** cassette series contains an edited version of the Learning to Do What Jesus Did Video Series (Product #41).

8 Audio Cassettes • $79 (plus shipping)

Walking Into a Life of Healing and Wholeness

Product #43	Awakening Your Spirit (audio cassette)

In this three tape audio series you will discover many ways to re-awaken your spirit and some of the ways the enemy has taken the joy of our salvation without us even knowing it. Also you will learn how to minister to those who have a wounded self-image or have made destructive inner vows. Includes the tapes *Breaking Inner Vows*, *Healing the Wounded Self Image*, and *Awakening Your Spirit*.

3 Audio Casettes • $15 (plus shipping)

Product #44	Healing Series (VHS video cassette)

Often, we go to God asking for His help or counsel. But then, when God does try to speak to us, we don't really want to hear what He has to say. Part of that is because we have barriers we've built that keep us from understanding our identity as sons and daughters of the King, and that we were *made* for intimacy with God. Also, we can be easily trapped by unforgiveness that brings Condemnation, Intimidation and Accusation. This can lead to feelings of inferiority, inadequacy, and self-rejection. This four tape video series helps you remove the barriers to intimacy with the Father, identify the traps of unforgiveness, and live in the freedom and power of our identity in Christ.

4 VHS Video Casettes • $79 (plus shipping)

To Order, Call
800-901-2025
Or Go To:
www.WasteTimeWithGod.org